FamilyCircle ®

Mince FABULOUS

RECIPES

The Family Circle® Promise of Success

Welcome to the world of Confident Cooking, created for you in the Australian **Family Circle® Test Kitchen,** where recipes are double-tested by our team of home economists to achieve a high standard of success—and delicious results every time.

M U R D O C H   B O O K S ®

Sydney • London • Vancouver • New York

C O N T E

Shepherd's Pie, page 16

Crepes with Spicy Mince and Lentils, page 32

Making Mince Fabulous	4
Family Favourites	6
Barbecued Sausages	26–27
Around the World	38
Sauces and Dips	56–57

Something Different	68
Party Pieces	78–81
Index	111
International Glossary of Ingredients	112

Prawn-filled Baby Eggplants, page 106

Chicken and Cheese Burgers, page 24

The test kitchen where our recipes are double-tested by our team of home economists to achieve a high standard of success and delicious results every time.

Chicken and Lemon Meatballs, page 13

Cottage Pie, page 34

The Publisher thanks the following for their assistance in the photography: Villeroy & Boch; Hummerston Gourmet Meats; Antico's Fruit World.
Front cover: Clockwise, from top left, Chilli con Carne, page 39; Meatballs with Tomato Garlic Sauce, page 22; Spicy Lamb Triangles, page 45; Beef Pie, page 6
Inside front cover: Cracked Wheat and Lamb Burger and Barbecued Tuna Burger, page 76

When we test our recipes, we rate them for ease of preparation. The following cookery ratings are on the recipes in this book, making them easy to use and understand.

A single Cooking with Confidence symbol indicates a recipe that is simple and generally quick to make —perfect for beginners.

Two symbols indicate the need for just a little more care and a little more time.

Three symbols indicate special dishes that need more investment in time, care and patience—but the results are worth it.

Larb, page 40

Mushroom, Mince and Feta Strudel, page 75

Making Mince Fabulous

Mince is the most versatile, and economical, cut of meat available. It absorbs flavours and seasonings wonderfully and is used throughout the world in an incredible variety of dishes. It is mince that is enjoyed by a Greek family when they sit down to a hearty moussaka; mince that is stuffed into small rice dumplings by a Chinese chef in a busy dim sum restaurant; and mince that has been elevated almost to a national symbol in the all-American hamburger. With a little imagination, and a little help from this book, turn your everyday mince into something fabulous.

Although most people instantly think 'beef' when they think of mince, in fact the word 'mince' refers to any meat, fish or seafood that has been finely chopped.

Beef mince does deserve its pre-eminent position. It is by far the most easily available mince and its popularity means you should always have a choice of different grades. Pick the right cut for your recipe (see our tips below) and what you will be taking home is an economical form of what can be an expensive meat. Add some fresh vegetables or pulses, and even a small amount can grow into a meal for a large and hungry family.

Though beef mince may be the foundation of many of our favourite family recipes (and we've included many of those traditional classics inside), there are also lots of great recipes using other kinds of mince. Chicken and lamb are familiar, but pork and veal mince, prawn or even fish can bring a new flavour and texture to a family recipe. Or try using these minces to make something a little different. The Asian Lemon Grass Prawn Satays are deliciously light and only take about 20 minutes to prepare.

BUYING FROM YOUR BUTCHER

Most butchers stock a variety of different mince grades. Plain ground beef, often called hamburger, is a mixture of several beef cuts and can contain as much as 30 percent fat. (Look at the amount of white marbling in the meat, this is the fat, and the more there is, the fattier the meat is.) Hamburger is the least expensive kind of mince, but don't forget that its

BROWNING MINCE

Make sure you brown your mince in small batches so that it has a chance to cook and brown evenly, rather than stewing over the heat. As it cooks, break up any lumps to give the meat a better texture and appearance.

Use a wooden spoon or fork to break up any lumps.

high fat content means it will shrink a lot when cooked. This grade of mince is therefore fine for dishes such as Lasagne but, despite its name, it's not the grade to choose if you want to make great hamburgers: your patties will just shrink too much when

To make your own mince, place chunks of the meat into a food processor.

Process in small bursts until the meat has the texture of mince.

Alternatively, use a sharp knife to chop the meat by hand.

cooked. A leaner mince is ground chuck steak, which has around 20 percent fat. This is one of the best and most useful beef minces, with just enough fat to give flavour, but not so much that your patties and meatballs shrivel up when cooked. This is the mince to go for when you want to make juicy, flavourful hamburgers and, when our recipes ask for 'lean beef mince', this grade is a good choice. A ground sirloin is often labelled as extra lean and can contain half as much fat as ordinary ground beef. This is the perfect grade for those watching their diet, but it can dry out if cooked for too long.

For other minces, such as chicken or lamb, the cut of meat doesn't matter so much and the fat content is naturally lower. Just make sure with all minces that your meat is as fresh as possible, and don't keep it in the refrigerator for more than 2 days.

When considering all these new leaner minces, remember that mince does need some fat. It adds greatly to the flavour, keeps the meat tender and stops it drying out. A very lean cut will dry out quickly if cooked for a long time. If you want to cut down on fat and cholesterol, try recipes where the meat is browned first; then you can drain off much of the fat from the frying pan.

MINCING YOUR OWN

Beef, pork, lamb and chicken mince are usually readily available from a good butcher. But if you want to use an unusual cut of meat, fish or perhaps some shellfish, you will probably need to buy the meat or seafood and mince it yourself.

To mince your own meat, place the trimmed meat in a food processor and process in short bursts. The result will be a mince with a smooth texture—ideal for sausages or hamburgers. Alternatively, make your own mince by chopping a fillet of lean meat or fish with a large, sharp knife. This method works particularly well for tender cuts, such as a fresh fish fillet or a small amount of a prime beef cut such as rump.

Mincing your own meat or fish allows you a lot more choice. You can make sure that your mince is

really fresh by picking the cut carefully at your butcher's and mincing it just before you want to use it. This also means that you can trim the sinew from your cut before you mince it. When you buy beef mince, the sinew has sometimes been minced along with the rest of the meat and this is what can cause even finely ground mince to taste a little tough.

Another bonus of mincing your own is if you want to cut down on the fat in your diet. It is often hard to tell how lean ready-made mince really is. Instead, buy your own cut of meat, trim the fat (remembering to

leave enough to keep the meat moist and flavourful) and mince the meat yourself. This way you can get exactly the quality of meat and leanness that you want.

It also allows you to get a really fine mince. A coarse mince works well for most dishes and prevents the meat becoming too bruised. However, for some dishes, such as meatballs and terrines, you need a really fine mince, which will hold together well and keep its shape better when cooked. If you have bought ready-made mince, you can chop it again at home to give it this finer texture.

WORKING WITH MINCE
MAKING PATTIES, MEATBALLS AND KOFTAS

When making patties, meatballs and koftas, it is important to make sure the meat is sticky enough to hold together well and keep its shape. However, you also want to prevent the meat becoming too compact, which means it will taste heavy when cooked. Follow the tips below to create light meatballs and patties that really work.

Mix together all the ingredients by hand. This helps the mince to come together and it will be less likely to fall apart during cooking.

You can mould the patties by hand or in egg rings. Wetting your hands first will make it easier to handle the meat.

When using skewers, mould the meat around the skewer, rather than threading it on. The meat will then stay together when cooked.

When you are grilling or cooking the patties, turn only once or twice, so that the meat doesn't dry out or fall apart.

FAMILY FAVOURITES

BEEF PIE

Preparation time: 35 minutes
+ 30 minutes refrigeration
Total cooking time: 1 hour
Serves 6

3/4 cup (90 g/3 oz) plain flour
1/3 cup (40 g/1 1/3 oz) self-raising
  flour
90 g (3 oz) butter, chopped
2 rashers rindless bacon,
  chopped
1 small onion, finely chopped
750 g (1 1/2 lb) lean beef mince
2 tablespoons plain flour, extra
1 1/2 cups (375 ml/12 fl oz) beef
  stock
1/2 cup (125 g/4 oz) tomato paste
2 tablespoons Worcestershire
  sauce
2 teaspoons dried mixed herbs
1 tablespoon dry mustard
375 g (12 oz) block frozen puff
  pastry
1 egg, lightly beaten

1 Mix the flours and butter in a food processor until fine and crumbly. Add 1 tablespoon of water and process until the mixture comes together, adding more water if necessary. Turn out onto a floured surface and gather it into a ball. Cover with plastic wrap and refrigerate for 30 minutes. Roll the pastry on a sheet of baking paper until large enough to cover the base and sides of a greased 23 cm (9 inch) round pie dish and refrigerate.

2 Heat some oil in a pan and cook the bacon and onion for 5 minutes. Add the beef mince and cook for 4 minutes, or until the liquid has evaporated and the meat browned. Use a fork to break up any lumps of mince as it cooks. Stir in the flour for 1 minute.

3 Add the stock, paste, sauce, herbs and mustard and bring to the boil. Reduce the heat and simmer, stirring occasionally, for 8 minutes, or until most of the liquid has evaporated. Cool, then place in the pastry shell. Preheat the oven to hot 210°C (415°F/Gas 6–7).

4 On a floured surface, roll out the puff pastry until it is large enough to cover the pie. Brush the edge of the pie shell with egg, place the pastry on top and trim the edges. Make cuts around the edge, cutting right through the pastry, and 4 cuts in the top. Brush with egg. Bake for 15 minutes. Reduce the heat to moderate 180°C (350°F/Gas 4) and bake for 25 minutes, or until golden.

Process the flours and butter until fine and crumbly.

Add the stock, tomato paste, sauce, herbs and mustard to the meat.

NACHOS

Preparation time: 30 minutes
Total cooking time: 25 minutes
Serves 4

400 g (12²/₃ oz) lean beef mince
1 onion, chopped
1–2 teaspoons chopped fresh
   chilli
1 tablespoon ground cumin
3 teaspoons ground coriander
¼ cup (60 g/2 oz) tomato paste
½ cup (125 g/4 oz) ready-made
   tomato pasta sauce or salsa
½ cup (115 g/3¾ oz) refried
   beans or 425 g (13½ oz) can
   red kidney beans, drained
corn chips, grated Cheddar cheese
   and sour cream, for serving

Guacamole
1 ripe avocado
1 small onion, finely chopped
1 tomato, finely chopped
2 tablespoons chopped fresh
   coriander
2–3 tablespoons sour cream
3–4 teaspoons lemon juice
Tabasco, to taste

1 Heat a little oil in a frying pan and brown the beef mince in batches, stirring and breaking up any lumps with a fork or wooden spoon. Transfer to a bowl and set aside.

2 Add a little more oil to the pan and stir in the onion, chilli, cumin and coriander. Cook over medium heat for 2–3 minutes. Return the mince to the pan and stir in the tomato paste and sauce and refried or kidney beans. Simmer for 5–10 minutes.

3 To make Guacamole: Peel the avocado and mash the flesh in a bowl.

Add the onion, tomato, coriander, sour cream and lemon juice. Mix well with a fork. Add some salt, freshly ground black pepper and Tabasco.

4 Spoon the mince into a large, ovenproof dish. Arrange the corn chips around the mixture and sprinkle

with the cheese. Place under a preheated grill or in a moderate 180°C (350°F/Gas 4) oven for about 5–10 minutes, or until the cheese has melted. Top with the Guacamole, a spoonful of sour cream and a dash of chilli powder.

Break up any lumps of mince with a fork or wooden spoon.

Stir in the tomato paste and sauce and the refried beans.

Add the onion, tomato, coriander, sour cream and lemon juice to the avocado.

HAMBURGER WITH THE WORKS

Preparation time: 20 minutes
Total cooking time: 15 minutes
Serves 4

500 g (1 lb) lean beef mince
1 onion, finely chopped
1 egg, lightly beaten
1/3 cup (25 g/3/4 oz) fresh
   breadcrumbs
2 tablespoons tomato sauce
1 teaspoon steak seasoning
40 g (11/3 oz) butter

2 onions, extra, cut in thin rings
4 slices Cheddar cheese, halved
4 eggs, extra
4 slices rindless bacon, halved
4 large hamburger buns, halved
shredded lettuce
1 large tomato, sliced
4 large beetroot slices, drained
4 pineapple rings, drained
tomato sauce, for serving

1 Place the beef mince, onion, egg, breadcrumbs, tomato sauce, steak seasoning and some salt and pepper in a large bowl. Use your hands to mix well. Divide into 4 portions and shape into round patties. Heat 30 g (1 oz) butter in a frying pan, add the onion rings and cook over medium heat until brown. Remove and keep warm.

2 Heat a frying pan or barbecue grill or flatplate and brush lightly with oil. Cook the patties for 3–4 minutes each side, or until cooked through. Place a cheese slice on each patty.

3 While the patties are cooking, heat the remaining butter in another frying pan and fry the eggs and the bacon separately. Toast the buns and top each one with lettuce, tomato, beetroot and pineapple. Add a meat patty and finish with some onion, egg and bacon.

Use your hands to mix the mince with the other ingredients.

Cook the patties for 3–4 minutes each side, or until cooked through.

Cook the bacon in a non-stick pan until it is crisp. Turn it over frequently.

SPAGHETTI BOLOGNESE

Preparation time: 20 minutes
Total cooking time: 1 hour 50 minutes
Serves 4–6

2 cloves garlic, crushed
1 large onion, chopped
1 carrot, finely chopped
1 celery stick, finely chopped
500 g (1 lb) lean beef mince
2 cups (500 ml/16 fl oz) beef
  stock

1¹/2 cups (375 ml/12 fl oz) red
  wine
2 x 425 g (13¹/2 oz) cans
  crushed tomatoes
1 teaspoon sugar
¹/4 cup (7 g/¹/4 oz) fresh parsley
  sprigs, finely chopped
500 g (1 lb) spaghetti
grated Parmesan, for serving

1 Heat some olive oil in a large, deep pan, add the garlic, onion, carrot and celery and stir over low heat for 5 minutes, or until just tender.

2 Increase the heat, add the mince and brown well, stirring and breaking up any lumps with a fork or wooden spoon. Add the stock, red wine, undrained tomatoes, sugar and parsley. Bring to the boil, reduce the heat and simmer for 1¹/2 hours, stirring occasionally. Season with salt and freshly ground black pepper.

3 Shortly before serving, cook the spaghetti in a large pan of rapidly boiling, salted water until just tender. Drain and serve with the meat sauce and the Parmesan.

Cook the garlic, onion, carrot and celery until they are just tender.

To the mince and vegetables, add the stock, wine, tomatoes, sugar and parsley.

Lower the spaghetti into a large pan of rapidly boiling water.

Combine the minces, onion, 1 egg, garlic, sauces, breadcrumbs and parsley.

On a board, cut the pastry sheets in half using a sharp knife.

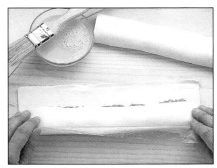

Carefully roll the pastry over the mixture and press the edges to seal.

Score the tops diagonally, being careful not to cut right through the pastry.

SAUSAGE ROLLS

Preparation time: 40 minutes
Total cooking time: 35 minutes
Makes 8

150 g (4³/4 oz) sausage mince
150 g (4³/4 oz) lean beef mince
1 small onion, finely chopped
    or grated
2 eggs
1–2 cloves garlic, crushed
1 tablespoon barbecue sauce
3 teaspoons Worcestershire
    sauce
¹/2 cup (40 g/1¹/3 oz) fresh
    breadcrumbs
2–3 tablespoons finely chopped
    fresh parsley
2 sheets ready-rolled puff
    pastry
tomato or chilli sauce,
    for serving

1 Preheat the oven to moderate 180°C (350°F/Gas 4). Line 2 baking trays with non-stick baking paper.
2 Using your hands, mix together the sausage and beef minces, onion, 1 egg, garlic, sauces, breadcrumbs, parsley and some salt and pepper.
3 Cut the pastry sheets in half and brush lightly with some of the remaining beaten egg. Divide the mince mixture into 4 equal portions and place 1 portion in a long sausage shape down the centre of each sheet.
4 Roll the pastry over the mixture and press the edges to seal, leaving the ends open. Use a sharp knife to cut the sausage rolls in half, then place on the trays, seam-side-down, ensuring there is enough room for them to spread. Brush with egg and lightly score the tops diagonally with a sharp knife. Bake for 35 minutes, or until crisp and golden. Serve with tomato or chilli sauce.

COOK'S FILE

Variation: Lightly sprinkle the rolls with poppy or sesame seeds after glazing with egg and before baking.

GOURMET MEATLOAF

Preparation time: 20 minutes
Total cooking time: 1 hour 15 minutes
Serves 4–6

500 g (1 lb) pork and veal mince
250 g (8 oz) sausage mince
1½ cups (120 g/3¾ oz) fresh
   white breadcrumbs
1 small green capsicum,
   chopped
1 medium onion, finely chopped

2 cloves garlic, crushed
½ cup (125 g/4 oz) ready-made
   chunky tomato sauce
½ cup (140 g/4²/3 oz) fruit
   chutney
1 egg, lightly beaten
½ cup (95 g/3¼ oz) chopped
   dried apricots
1 tablespoon green peppercorns,
   drained, chopped
2 tablespoons chopped fresh mint
2 teaspoons sweet paprika
1 tablespoon toasted sesame
   seeds

1 Brush a 23 x 13 cm (9 x 4¾ inch) loaf tin lightly with oil. Preheat the oven to moderate 180°C (350°F/Gas 4).
2 Combine the minces in a bowl. Add the breadcrumbs, capsicum, onion, garlic, tomato sauce, chutney, egg, apricot, peppercorns, mint and paprika and mix together well.
3 Press into the tin and place on an oven tray to catch any juices that spill over. Bake for 1 hour 15 minutes. Carefully pour off the juices, turn out the meatloaf and sprinkle with sesame seeds. Serve with extra fruit chutney.

Use a large, sharp knife to chop the green peppercorns.

Use your hands to thoroughly combine the meat with the other ingredients.

Press the meat mixture into the prepared loaf tin.

CHICKEN AND LEMON MEATBALLS

Preparation time: 20 minutes
+ 30 minutes refrigeration
Total cooking time: 10 minutes
Serves 4

500 g (1 lb) chicken mince
2 cloves garlic, crushed
1 cup (80 g/2²/3 oz) fresh white
    breadcrumbs
1 teaspoon grated lemon rind

1 teaspoon fresh lemon thyme
    leaves
1 egg, lightly beaten
1 tablespoon olive oil
2 tablespoons lemon juice

Yoghurt Mint Sauce
200 g (6¹/2 oz) plain yoghurt
1 tablespoon shredded fresh mint
rinsed, chopped skin from
    ¹/4 of a preserved lemon

1 Using your hands, mix together the chicken mince, garlic, breadcrumbs, lemon rind, thyme, egg and some salt and black pepper. Wet your hands and form tablespoons of the mixture into balls and place on a lined tray. Refrigerate for 30 minutes.
2 To make Yoghurt Mint Sauce: Mix together all the ingredients.
3 Heat the oil in a non-stick frying pan and cook the meatballs in 2 batches, until golden on all sides and cooked through. Sprinkle with lemon juice, transfer to a serving dish and sprinkle with more salt. Serve with Yoghurt Mint Sauce.

Combine the chicken, garlic, breadcrumbs, lemon rind, thyme, egg, salt and pepper.

Using wet hands, roll tablespoons of the mixture into balls.

Cook the meatballs in batches until golden and cooked through.

13

CHICKEN AND LEEK PIE

Preparation time: 20 minutes
Total cooking time: 35–40 minutes
Serves 4–6

2 tablespoons oil
2 medium leeks, finely
   sliced
500 g (1 lb) chicken mince
2 tablespoons plain flour
1 cup (250 ml/8 fl oz) cream
1/4 cup (60 ml/2 fl oz) water
1/2 cup (125 ml/4 fl oz) chicken
   stock

440 g (14 oz) can corn kernels,
   drained
3 tablespoons chopped fresh
   parsley
2 sheets ready-rolled puff
   pastry, thawed
1 egg, lightly beaten
2 teaspoons sesame seeds

1 Preheat the oven to hot 210°C (415°F/Gas 6–7). Lightly brush a shallow 20 by 25 cm (8 by 10 inch) casserole dish with melted butter. Heat the oil in a pan, add the leek and cook, stirring, for 5 minutes, or until softened. Add the chicken mince and stir for 5 minutes, or until just cooked, breaking up any lumps with a fork.

2 Sprinkle the mince with flour and mix well. Add the cream and water and stir over low heat until the mixture boils and thickens. Add the chicken stock, corn and parsley. Season with salt and pepper. Spoon the mixture into the casserole dish.

3 Lay 1 sheet of pastry on a work surface, brush with egg and top with the other sheet. Put on top of the pie, trim or roll the edges and mark with a sharp knife. Cut 3 steam holes in the top. Brush with egg, sprinkle with sesame seeds and bake for 20 minutes.

Stir the leeks for 5 minutes, or until they become soft.

Add the chicken stock, corn and parsley to the pan.

After brushing one sheet of pastry with egg, top with another sheet.

GOULASH SOUP

Preparation time: 20 minutes
Total cooking time: 40 minutes
Serves 4

1 tablespoon oil
1 large onion, chopped
300 g (92/3 oz) lean beef mince
2 cloves garlic, chopped
3 teaspoons sweet paprika
11/2 teaspoons caraway seeds
1 tablespoon tomato paste

3 cups (750 ml/24 fl oz) beef or
   vegetable stock
1/2 red capsicum, seeded and
   finely diced
1 celery stick, finely diced
2 tablespoons finely chopped
   fresh parsley
sour cream, for serving

1 Heat the oil in a pan and cook the onion until soft. Increase the heat, add the beef mince and cook until brown, breaking up any lumps with a fork or wooden spoon.

2 Reduce the heat and add the garlic, paprika and seeds. Cook for a minute, then add the paste, stock, capsicum and celery. Bring to the boil, lower the heat and simmer for 30 minutes.

3 Stir in the parsley and spoon into warm bowls. Swirl in a spoonful of sour cream and sprinkle over some extra parsley.

C O O K ' S   F I L E

Note: You can make this soup a few days in advance and refrigerate. This will allow the flavours to develop.

When the onions have softened, increase the heat to high and add the mince.

Reduce the heat and add the garlic, sweet paprika and caraway seeds to the meat.

Stir in the chopped parsley just before spooning the soup into warm bowls.

Chicken and Leek Pie (top)
with Goulash Soup

SHEPHERD'S PIE

Preparation time: 30 minutes
Total cooking time: 1 hour
Serves 4–6

750 g (1¹/2 lb) lean cooked lamb
25 g (³/4 oz) butter
2 onions, thinly sliced
¹/4 cup (30 g/1 oz) plain flour
¹/2 teaspoon dry mustard
1¹/2 cups (375 ml/12 fl oz)
   chicken stock
2 tablespoons chopped fresh
   mint

1 tablespoon chopped fresh
   parsley
2 tablespoons Worcestershire
   sauce

Potato Topping
4 large potatoes, cooked
¹/4 cup (60 ml/2 fl oz) hot milk
30 g (1 oz) butter

1 Brush an 8-cup capacity ovenproof dish with melted butter or oil. Preheat the oven to hot 210°C (415°F/Gas 6–7). Trim the meat and mince finely with a sharp knife. Melt the butter in a pan, add the onion and cook until brown.

Sprinkle with flour and mustard.
2 Gradually add the stock and stir until smooth. Bring to the boil, reduce the heat and simmer for 3 minutes. Stir in the lamb mince, mint, parsley, Worcestershire sauce and some salt and black pepper. Spoon the mixture into the dish.
3 To make Potato Topping: Mash the potatoes slightly and then add the milk, butter and some salt and pepper. Mash until the potato is smooth and creamy, adding more milk if necessary. Pipe or spread over the meat and bake for 40–45 minutes, or until the potato is golden.

Using a sharp knife, finely chop the lean cooked lamb until minced.

Gradually add the stock and stir with a wooden spoon until smooth.

Mash the potatoes and mix with the milk, butter, salt and pepper until smooth.

RISSOLES WITH GRAVY

Preparation time: 40 minutes
Total cooking time: 15–20 minutes
Makes 10

500 g (1 lb) lean beef mince
1 onion, finely chopped
2 cloves garlic, crushed
2 tablespoons tomato paste
    or sauce
2–3 teaspoons Dijon mustard
2 tablespoons chopped fresh
    parsley
1 tablespoon chopped fresh
    lemon thyme or chives
2 eggs
flour, for dusting
milk
1 cup (100 g/3¹/₃ oz) dried
    breadcrumbs

Gravy
1 tablespoon plain flour
1 cup (250 ml/8 fl oz) beef or
    vegetable stock
¹/₄ cup (60 ml/2 fl oz) red wine

1 Using your hands, combine the beef mince, onion, garlic, tomato paste or sauce, mustard, herbs and 1 beaten egg in a large bowl. Season with salt and freshly ground black pepper. Shape into patties by pressing small handfuls of the mixture into floured egg rings. Press down with your hand to flatten the patties, then remove the egg ring and lightly dust each patty with flour.
2 Whisk the remaining egg with a little milk. Dip the patties, one at a time, into the egg mixture and then coat in breadcrumbs, gently pressing so that the breadcrumbs stick. Heat a little oil in a large frying pan. Cook the rissoles in batches, over medium heat, for 3–4 minutes each side, or until cooked through and well browned. Remove from the pan, cover and keep warm.
3 **To make Gravy:** Drain any excess oil from the pan, leaving about 2–3 teaspoons. Add the flour and stir for 1 minute. Gradually blend in the combined stock and red wine, stirring to incorporate the bits from the base of the pan. Stir constantly, over medium heat, until the sauce boils and thickens. Simmer for 2–3 minutes and season with salt and pepper. Pour the gravy over the rissoles and serve.

Shape into patties by pressing small amounts of mixture into floured egg rings.

Dip each patty into the egg and then press into the breadcrumbs.

Slowly add the combined stock and red wine, stirring continuously.

PORK TERRINE

Preparation time: 25 minutes
  + overnight refrigeration
Total cooking time: 1 hour 10 minutes
Serves 6–8

14 thick slices prosciutto
750 g (1¹/₂ lb) lean pork mince
250 g (8 oz) sausage mince
¹/₂ cup (60 g/2 oz) slivered
    almonds, toasted
1 tablespoon sambal oelek
2 teaspoons ground cumin
2 teaspoons sesame oil
1 tablespoon lemon thyme leaves

Plum Relish
825 g (1 lb 11 oz) can plums
250 g (8 oz) jar cranberry sauce
2 tablespoons sweet chilli sauce
2 teaspoons grated lime rind

1 Preheat the oven to moderate 180°C (350°F/Gas 4). Line a 6-cup capacity loaf tin or dish with prosciutto, overlapping the slices and leaving the ends hanging over the edge. Make sure you line all of the dish.
2 In a large bowl, combine the pork and sausage mince, almonds, sambal oelek, cumin, sesame oil, thyme leaves, 1 teaspoon of salt and a little cracked pepper. Mix well with your hands.

3 Press the mince mixture firmly into the tin. Fold the prosciutto slices over the top of the filling and cover with foil. Place the terrine inside a baking dish and pour in boiling water to come halfway up the sides of the tin. Bake for 1 hour 10 minutes, or until the terrine is firm.
4 Carefully pour off the juices and cool. Cover with plastic wrap and foil and refrigerate overnight. Turn out onto a plate and slice.
5 **To make Plum Relish:** Chop the drained plums and discard the stones. Mix in the cranberry sauce, sweet chilli sauce and lime rind. Serve hot or cold with the terrine.

Line the pan, including corners and ends, with prosciutto, leaving slices overhanging.

Level the top of the mince and fold the ends of the prosciutto over the filling.

Drain and then chop the plums, discarding the stones.

SPICY LAMB CURRY

Preparation time: 30 minutes
Total cooking time: 40 minutes
Serves 4

750 g (1½ lb) lean lamb mince
1 tablespoon soy sauce
2 tablespoons chopped fresh
   coriander
2 tablespoons oil
2 large onions, sliced
2 teaspoons grated fresh ginger
2 garlic cloves, crushed
2 red chillies, chopped
6 curry leaves

1 teaspoon ground cinnamon
2 teaspoons ground turmeric
2 teaspoons grated lemon rind
1 tablespoon tamarind sauce
1 tablespoon white vinegar
3 tablespoons fruit or mango
   chutney
1½ cups (375 ml/12 fl oz) water

1 Mix together the lamb mince, soy sauce and coriander. Roll tablespoons of the mixture into balls. Heat the oil in a heavy-based frying pan. Cook the lamb balls, in batches, over medium heat for 4 minutes, or until brown, turning occasionally. Remove and drain on paper towels.

2 Add the onion, ginger, garlic and chilli to the pan and stir-fry over medium heat for 2 minutes, or until the onion is tender.

3 Add the curry leaves, cinnamon, turmeric, lemon rind, tamarind sauce, vinegar, chutney and water to the pan; bring to the boil. Return the lamb meatballs to the pan, reduce the heat and simmer, covered, for 15 minutes, or until the sauce has reduced and thickened, stirring occasionally.

COOK'S FILE

Note: Make this curry up to 2 days in advance for the flavours to develop. Store, covered, in the refrigerator.

Remove the meatballs from the pan and drain on paper towels.

Stir the onions over medium heat until they are tender.

Add curry leaves, spices, lemon rind, tamarind, vinegar, chutney and water.

PISTACHIO AND PORK STUFFED TURKEY

Preparation time: 45 minutes
Total cooking time: 3 hours
Serves 12

5 kg (10 lb) turkey, fresh or
    completely thawed
1 m (3¹/₃ ft) square of muslin,
    washed and dried
¹/₂ cup (125 ml/4 fl oz) olive oil
125 g (4 oz) butter, melted

Pistachio Stuffing
2 tablespoons olive oil
1 onion, finely chopped
100 g (3¹/₃ oz) pistachios,
    shelled and chopped
100 g (3¹/₃ oz) currants
1 tablespoon finely grated lemon
    rind
¹/₃ cup (80 ml/2³/₄ fl oz) lemon
    juice
3 cups (240 g/7¹/₂ oz) fresh
    white breadcrumbs

Forcemeat Stuffing
60 g (2 oz) butter
6 spring onions, chopped
¹/₃ cup (80 ml/2³/₄ fl oz) white
    wine vinegar
2 tablespoons green
    peppercorns
400 g (12²/₃ oz) pork mince
1 egg, lightly beaten

Gravy
¹/₄ cup (30 g/1 oz) plain flour
1¹/₂ cups (375 ml/12 fl oz)
    chicken stock
¹/₂ cup (125 ml/4 fl oz) white
    wine
¹/₄ cup (60 ml/ 2 fl oz) sweet
    sherry

1 Preheat the oven to moderate 180°C (350°F/Gas 4). Remove the giblets, wash inside the turkey with cold running water and pat dry with paper towels. Soak the muslin in the combined oil and butter.

2 To make Pistachio Stuffing: Heat the oil in a pan, add the onion and cook for 1–2 minutes. Transfer to a bowl and mix with the remaining ingredients. Spoon into the cavity and secure the opening with a skewer.

3 To make Forcemeat Stuffing: Heat the butter in a pan, add the spring onion and cook for 2 minutes. Add the vinegar and peppercorns and simmer for 5 minutes. Transfer to a bowl, add the remaining ingredients and mix. Spoon half the stuffing under the skin at the neck end and secure the opening with a skewer. Tie the legs together with string. Roll the remaining mixture into small balls. Pan-fry in a little oil until browned.

4 Place the turkey on a roasting rack in a baking dish. Add ¹/₂ cup (125 ml/4 fl oz) water to the dish. Wrap the prepared muslin around the turkey. Cover the entire bird and dish with foil. Bake for 2 hours.

5 Remove the foil and muslin. Cook for another 30–60 minutes, brushing the juices over the turkey every 15 minutes. Remove from the pan, cover with foil and set aside.

6 To make Gravy: Remove all but 3 tablespoons of the juices from the baking dish, add the flour and mix. Cook for 4 minutes, or until the mixture is golden, stirring often. Remove from the heat and gradually add the combined liquids. Return to the heat and stir until the gravy boils and thickens. Season with salt and pepper. Serve with the turkey and the reheated meatballs.

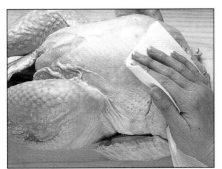

Pat the washed turkey dry with some paper towels.

Spoon the Pistachio Stuffing into the cavity.

Spoon the Forcemeat Stuffing under the skin at the neck.

Use kitchen string to tie together the turkey legs.

Place the turkey on a rack in the baking dish and add water to the dish.

Wrap the prepared muslin around the turkey, covering the whole bird.

MEATBALLS WITH TOMATO GARLIC SAUCE

Preparation time: 40 minutes
Total cooking time: 1 hour 30 minutes
Serves 4

500 g (1 lb) veal mince
1 onion, grated
1 cup (80 g/2²/3 oz) fresh white
    breadcrumbs
2 tablespoons sun-dried
    tomatoes, finely chopped
1 egg, lightly beaten
olive oil
400 g (12²/3 oz) pasta

Tomato Garlic Sauce
25 g (³/4 oz) butter
1 onion, finely chopped
2–3 cloves garlic, crushed
2 teaspoons plain flour
425 g (13¹/2 oz) can crushed
    tomatoes
1 tablespoon tomato paste
³/4 cup (185 ml/6 fl oz) chicken
    stock
1 tablespoon chopped fresh
    oregano
1 teaspoon sugar

1 Using your hands, mix together the veal mince, onion, breadcrumbs, sun-dried tomatoes, egg and some salt and pepper. Roll tablespoons of the mixture into balls. Heat some oil in a frying pan and brown the meatballs in batches. Place in a casserole dish. Preheat the oven to moderate 180°C (350°F/Gas 4).

2 To make Tomato Garlic Sauce: In the same frying pan, melt the butter and cook the onion until soft. Add the garlic and flour and cook for 1 minute. Stir in the tomatoes, tomato paste, stock, oregano, sugar and some salt and pepper. Cook for 2 minutes. Pour the sauce over the meatballs in the dish, cover and bake for 1 hour.

3 Cook the pasta in a pan of boiling water for approximately 10 minutes, or until just tender. Drain and serve with the meatballs.

Use your hands to combine the meat with the other ingredients in the bowl.

Use tongs to turn the meatballs frequently until brown all over.

Stir in the tomatoes, tomato paste, stock, oregano, sugar, salt and pepper.

Use a wooden spoon or fork to break up any lumps of meat.

Stir the onion over medium heat until it turns golden.

Simmer until the liquid reduces and the sauce has thickened.

Brush the combined oil and garlic over each slice of bread.

SAVOURY MINCE

Preparation time: 25 minutes
Total cooking time: 25 minutes
Serves 4–6

3 tablespoons oil
30 g (1 oz) butter
500 g (1 lb) lean beef mince
1 onion, chopped
1 large carrot, grated
1/3 cup (80 ml/2³/4 fl oz) tomato
   sauce
1/3 cup (80 ml/2³/4 fl oz) beef
   or vegetable stock
2 teaspoons Dijon or English
   mustard
2 tablespoons chopped fresh
   parsley
1–2 cloves garlic, crushed
crusty bread slices

1 Heat about 2 teaspoons of the oil and half the butter in a large frying pan. Add the beef mince in batches and stir constantly, over high heat, until well browned, breaking up any lumps with a fork or wooden spoon. Transfer the mince to a bowl and set aside.

2 Add the remaining butter and 2 teaspoons of oil to the pan. Stir in the onion and cook over medium heat for 3–4 minutes, or until golden.

3 Return the meat to the pan and stir in the carrot, tomato sauce, stock and mustard. Reduce the heat and simmer the sauce for 5–10 minutes, or until the liquid has reduced and the sauce thickened. Stir in the parsley and season, to taste, with salt and freshly ground black pepper.

4 Combine the remaining oil with the crushed garlic and brush over each slice of bread. Place the bread under a preheated grill and toast each side until golden. Spoon the mince over the toast and serve.

CHICKEN AND CHEESE BURGERS

Preparation time: 40 minutes
Total cooking time:10–15 minutes
Makes 6

1 large onion, finely chopped
750 g (1½ lb) chicken mince
1 teaspoon paprika
1–2 teaspoons chopped fresh
    chilli
¾ cup (60 g/2 oz) fresh
    breadcrumbs
⅓ cup (90 g/3 oz) sour cream
2 tablespoons chopped fresh
    lemon thyme or chives
90 g (3 oz) Cheddar cheese

30 g (1 oz) butter
1–2 cloves garlic, crushed
6 crusty bread rolls
lettuce, tomato, extra sour
    cream, pickled cucumbers
    and sweet chilli sauce, for
    serving

1 Heat a little oil in a frying pan. Add the onion and cook over medium heat until golden. Drain the onion on paper towels and cool slightly.
2 Using your hands, mix together in a large bowl the onion, chicken mince, paprika, chilli, breadcrumbs, sour cream, lemon thyme or chives and some salt and freshly ground black pepper. Divide the mixture into 6 equal portions and shape into round

balls. Cut the cheese into 6 pieces. Press a piece of cheese into the centre of each ball and mould the mixture to completely enclose the cheese. Flatten the balls slightly to make patties.
3 Heat the butter and 1 tablespoon of oil in a large frying pan. Add the garlic. When the mixture is foaming, add the patties, pressing with a spatula to flatten slightly. Cook over medium heat for 2–3 minutes each side, or until the patties are browned and the cheese melted.
4 Split the bread rolls in half. Toast and spread with a little butter if you wish. Fill with lettuce and tomato slices, a chicken patty, sour cream, some pickled cucumbers and sweet chilli sauce.

Transfer the cooked onion to a plate covered with paper towels, to drain.

Press a portion of cheese into the centre of each ball and completely enclose.

When the mixture is foaming, add the patties to the pan.

PIZZA WITH RED CAPSICUM AND BEEF

Preparation time: 35 minutes
Total cooking time: 30 minutes
Serves 2–4

1 small red capsicum
1 large ready-made
    pizza base
2–3 tablespoons tomato paste
1 clove garlic, crushed
1/2 teaspoon sweet paprika
1 red onion, thinly sliced
1 teaspoon olive oil
125 g (4 oz) lean beef mince

10 Kalamata olives, pitted and
    roughly chopped
1 tablespoon fresh oregano
    leaves
1 fresh red chilli, finely
    sliced
1 cup (150 g/4³/4 oz) grated
    mozzarella cheese

1 Cut the capsicum into large pieces, removing the seeds and membrane and brush the skin lightly with some oil. Grill, skin-side-up, until the skin blisters and blackens. Seal in a plastic bag, or cover with a damp tea towel, until cool. Remove the skin and slice the flesh thinly.

2 Preheat the oven to moderately hot 200°C (400°F/Gas 6). Place the pizza base on a baking tray and spread with the combined tomato paste, garlic and paprika. Sprinkle with the red capsicum and onion.

3 Heat the oil in a frying pan and brown the beef mince well, breaking up any lumps with a fork or wooden spoon. Season with some salt and freshly ground black pepper.

4 Sprinkle the beef over the pizza and scatter with the olives, oregano leaves and chilli. Top with the mozzarella. Bake for 20 minutes, or until the base is crisp and the cheese has melted. Cut into wedges to serve.

Remove the seeds and membrane from the capsicum.

Combine the tomato paste, garlic and paprika and spread over the pizza base.

Sprinkle the beef over the top of the red capsicum and onion.

Barbecued Sausages

Sausages are made from finely minced meat, usually pork or beef, mixed with cereal or bread seasonings and packed into a tube-shaped casing. They now come in an enticing variety of gourmet flavours—from sun-dried tomato to garlic and herb, and from spicy lamb to kangaroo meat.

These sausages need no enhancement, just cook and serve with a salad or some vegetables. But for creative cooks who want their traditional beef or pork sausages to take pride of place on their barbecue menu, a simple marinade or baste can change an ordinary sausage into something extra special.

Marinades add flavour to meat or vegetables, and when they have an acid ingredient such as lemon juice, wine or vinegar, they also work to tenderize the meat. Leave the sausages in the marinade for several hours or overnight to give them time to absorb the flavours of the marinade. The longer you leave them—the more intense the flavours will be when the sausages are cooked.

A baste is similar to a marinade, but is brushed over the food while it cooks. The result is a lovely, subtle flavour. Basting is also a great way of keeping the sausages moist while they cook on the barbecue.

The following recipes make enough marinade for about 12 sausages. To use as a baste, brush the mixture over the sausages while they are cooking, rather than marinating the sausages first.

FRESH HERB MARINADE

Mix the following ingredients thoroughly in a bowl: 1/4 cup (60 ml/2 fl oz) olive oil, 2–3 tablespoons lemon juice or balsamic vinegar, 1–2 crushed cloves garlic, 3 teaspoons soft brown sugar, some salt and freshly ground black pepper and 4 tablespoons of chopped fresh mixed herbs (use any combination you wish—chives, lemon thyme, rosemary, parsley, basil, coriander, mint, oregano or marjoram). Prick the sausages all over and marinate, covered, for at least 3 hours or overnight in the refrigerator. Turn the sausages occasionally. Use with any type of sausage. This mixture is also suitable for basting.

HONEY AND CHILLI MARINADE

Mix the following ingredients thoroughly in a bowl: 1/4 cup (60 ml/2 fl oz) soy sauce, 1 tablespoon grated fresh ginger, 2 teaspoons grated lemon rind, 1/4 cup (90 g/3 oz) honey, 1–2 crushed cloves garlic, 1 tablespoon sherry or rice wine and 3 tablespoons sweet chilli sauce. Prick the sausages all over and marinate, covered, for at least 3 hours or overnight in the refrigerator. Turn the sausages occasionally. This marinade goes well with any kind of sausage. It is also suitable for basting.

SPICY TANDOORI MARINADE

Mix the following ingredients thoroughly in a bowl: 1 tablespoon oil, 2 teaspoons each of ground cumin, coriander and paprika, 3 teaspoons turmeric, 2 teaspoons each of fresh grated ginger and tamarind sauce, 2 crushed cloves garlic, 1/2–1 teaspoon chilli powder, 1/2 teaspoon salt, 3 tablespoons tomato sauce and 200 g (6 1/2 oz) plain yoghurt. Prick the sausages all over and marinate, covered, for at least 3 hours or overnight in the refrigerator. Turn the sausages occasionally. Use for lamb or chicken sausages. This mixture is also suitable for basting.
Note: You can use a commercial tandoori paste or powder if you prefer.

PLUM AND CORIANDER MARINADE

Mix the following ingredients thoroughly in a bowl: 1/4 cup (60 ml/2 fl oz) plum sauce, 1–2 crushed cloves garlic, 1 tablespoon each of Worcestershire and soy sauce, 2 tablespoons each of lime juice and chopped fresh coriander and 1/4 cup (60 ml/2 fl oz) tomato sauce. Prick the sausages all over and marinate, covered, for at least 3 hours or overnight in the refrigerator. Turn the sausages occasionally. This mixture is also suitable for basting.

APRICOT AND ONION MARINADE

Mix the following ingredients thoroughly in a bowl: 1/3 cup (80 ml/2 3/4 fl oz) apricot nectar, 3 tablespoons lime marmalade, 2 crushed cloves garlic, 2 tablespoons olive oil, 1–2 tablespoons French onion soup mix, 1 tablespoon chopped fresh chives, a dash of Worcestershire sauce. Prick the sausages all over and marinate, covered, for at least 3 hours or overnight in the refrigerator. Turn the sausages occasionally. This mixture is also suitable for basting.

Marinades, clockwise, from top left: Fresh Herb; Honey and Chilli; Spicy Tandoori; Plum and Coriander; Apricot and Onion

BEEFY POTATO SKINS WITH GUACAMOLE

Preparation time: 30 minutes
Total cooking time: 1 hour 50 minutes
Serves 4

4 medium potatoes
4 tablespoons olive oil
600 g (1¼ lb) lean beef mince
1 medium onion, sliced
¼ cup (60 ml/2 fl oz) barbecue
   sauce
2 tablespoons tomato sauce

Guacamole
2 medium avocados
2 tablespoons lemon juice
1 small onion, finely chopped
1 small tomato, finely chopped
5 drops Tabasco, or to taste

1 Preheat the oven to hot 210°C (415°F/Gas 6–7). Scrub the potatoes under running water and prick all over with a fork or skewer. Bake in the oven for 1 hour. Remove and cut in half. With a metal spoon, remove the cooked potato from the centre, leaving a 1 cm (½ inch)-thick shell. Brush all over with 3 tablespoons of the oil, place on a tray and return to the oven for 30 minutes.
2 Heat the remaining oil in a heavy-based pan and add the mince and onion. Cook over medium heat for 10 minutes, or until the meat has browned and almost all the liquid has evaporated. Use a fork or wooden spoon to break up any lumps of mince as it cooks. Reduce the heat to low, add the barbecue and tomato sauces and simmer for another 10 minutes.
3 To make Guacamole: Mash the avocado flesh with a fork until almost smooth and mix in the remaining ingredients. Refrigerate until required.
4 Place 2 potato halves on each plate and fill with the mince mixture. Top with Guacamole and serve with salad.

COOK'S FILE

Note: The leftover potato can be mashed with a little milk and butter and placed back in the potato skins after baking. Pile the beef mince and Guacamole on top. Alternatively, you can use it as a topping for a cottage or shepherd's pie.

Use a brush to scrub the potatoes under running water.

Remove the cooked potato from the centre, leaving a shell.

Cook over medium heat until the meat has browned and the liquid evaporated.

Put the avocado flesh in a bowl and mash with a fork until almost smooth.

TANDOORI CHICKEN TERRINE

Preparation time: 20 minutes +
  overnight refrigeration
Total cooking time: 1 hour 30 minutes
Serves 6–8

8 slices bacon, rind removed
30 g (1 oz) butter
1 medium onion, finely chopped
2 cloves garlic, crushed
1 teaspoon grated fresh ginger
1 kg (2 lb) chicken mince
250 g (8 oz) chicken livers
1 teaspoon turmeric

1 teaspoon sweet paprika
1 teaspoon garam masala
1/2 teaspoon ground cardamom
1 teaspoon ground coriander
2 tablespoons lemon juice
1 cup (250 g/8 oz) plain yoghurt
2 eggs, lightly beaten

1 Preheat the oven to moderate 180°C (350°F/Gas 4). Lightly oil a 27 x 10 cm (11 x 4 inch) terrine dish or tin and line with bacon, overlapping the sides of the dish. Melt the butter in a pan, add the onion, garlic and ginger and fry for 2–3 minutes. Remove from heat.
2 Finely mince the chicken mince and livers in a food processor.

Transfer to a large bowl and add the onion mixture, spices and lemon juice.
3 Whisk the yoghurt and eggs and stir into the chicken mixture. Spoon into the dish, pressing down firmly. Fold the bacon over the top of the terrine to enclose the mixture, cover with foil and place in a baking dish.
4 Pour in enough cold water to come halfway up the terrine's sides. Bake for 1–1½ hours, or until the juices run clear when pierced with a skewer.
5 Remove from the oven and water bath and pour off the excess juice. Cover with foil and place a heavy weight on top of the terrine mixture to compress it. Refrigerate overnight.

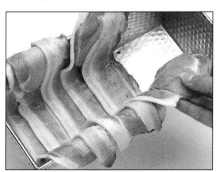

Line the dish with bacon, leaving the ends overlapping the sides of the dish.

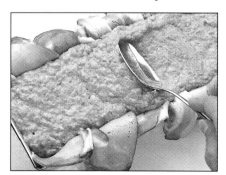

Spread the chicken mixture over the bacon, pressing down firmly.

Pour in enough cold water to come halfway up the sides of the terrine dish.

MEATBALL STROGANOFF

Preparation time: 40 minutes
Total cooking time: 20–25 minutes
Serves 4

750 g (1¹/₂ lb) lean beef mince
2 cloves garlic, crushed
2–3 tablespoons plain flour
¹/₂ teaspoon ground black
    pepper
1 teaspoon sweet paprika
2 tablespoons oil
50 g (1²/₃ oz) butter
1 large onion, thinly sliced
250 g (8 oz) small button
    mushrooms, halved
2 tablespoons tomato paste
2–3 teaspoons Dijon mustard
¹/₄ cup (60 ml/2 fl oz) white
    wine
¹/₂ cup (125 ml/4 fl oz) beef
    stock
³/₄ cup (185 g/6 oz) sour cream
3 tablespoons finely chopped
    fresh parsley

1 Combine the beef mince, garlic and some salt and cracked pepper in a bowl. Use your hands to mix well. Roll 2 heaped teaspoons of the mince into balls. Combine the flour, pepper and paprika on a clean surface or sheet of greaseproof paper. Dust the meatballs in the seasoned flour.

2 Heat the oil and half the butter in a frying pan. When foaming, cook the meatballs over medium heat, in batches, until brown. Remove from the pan and drain on paper towels.

3 Melt the remaining butter in the pan and add the onion. Cook for 2–3 minutes, or until soft. Stir in the mushrooms and continue cooking until the mushrooms are tender.

Pour in the combined tomato paste, mustard, wine and stock. Return the meatballs to the pan and gently reheat. Bring the mixture to the boil, reduce the heat and simmer for

5 minutes, stirring occasionally. Season to taste with salt and pepper. Stir the sour cream through until smooth. Sprinkle over a little parsley and serve with noodles.

Roll the meatballs in the flour mixture until lightly coated.

Brown the meatballs in batches so that they fry rather than stew.

Pour in the combined tomato paste, mustard, wine and stock.

BEEF AND EGGPLANT WITH FILO TOPPING

Preparation time: 45 minutes
Total cooking time: 50–55 minutes
Serves 4

2 tablespoons olive oil
1 large onion, finely chopped
200 g (6½ oz) eggplant, cubed
1 celery stick, thinly sliced
400 g (12⅔ oz) lean beef mince
1 tablespoon plain flour
1½ cups (375 ml/12 fl oz) beef stock
⅓ cup (80 ml/2¾ fl oz) red or white wine

1½ tablespoons tomato paste
6 Kalamata olives, pitted and chopped
2–3 teaspoons fresh thyme leaves
6–8 sheets filo pastry
melted butter, for brushing

1 Heat 1 tablespoon of oil in a frying pan. Add the onion and cook until golden. Add another 2 teaspoons of oil, stir in the eggplant and celery and cook for about 5 minutes, or until the eggplant is soft. Remove all the vegetables and set aside.

2 Add the remaining 2 teaspoons of oil to the pan and brown the mince, breaking up any lumps with a fork or wooden spoon. Add the flour and cook for 1 minute. Remove from the heat and stir in the stock, wine and tomato paste. Return to the heat and add the vegetables, olives and thyme and simmer for 20 minutes. Season, to taste. Place the beef and eggplant mixture in an 8-cup capacity casserole dish. Preheat the oven to moderately hot 200°C (400°F/Gas 6).

3 Cover the filo pastry with a damp tea towel and work with 1 sheet at a time to prevent the pastry drying out. Brush the sheets with melted butter and loosely scrunch up with your fingers. Arrange on top of the beef mixture until completely covered. Bake for 20 minutes, or until golden brown on top.

Add the eggplant and celery to the onion in the pan and cook for about 5 minutes.

Remove the pan from the heat and stir in the stock, wine and tomato paste.

Loosely scrunch up the buttered filo with your fingers and arrange over the beef.

CREPES WITH SPICY MINCE AND LENTILS

Preparation time: 45 minutes
+ 30 minutes standing
Total cooking time: 1 hour 20 minutes
Serves 4

1 cup (125 g/4 oz) plain flour
50 g (1²/3 oz) melted butter
   or 2 tablespoons oil
2 eggs, lightly beaten
2¹/4 cups (560 ml/18 fl oz) milk
³/4 cup (90 g/3 oz) grated
   Cheddar cheese

Filling
1 tablespoon oil
1 large onion, finely chopped
300 g (9²/3 oz) lean beef mince
2 cloves garlic, crushed
1 teaspoon chilli powder
1 teaspoon spicy paprika
425 g (13¹/2 oz) can chopped
   tomatoes
1 cup (250 ml/8 fl oz) chicken
   stock
200 g (6¹/2 oz) red lentils
2 teaspoons sugar
1 tablespoon wine vinegar

1 Sift the flour into a bowl, make a well in the centre and gradually pour in the combined butter or oil, eggs and milk, whisking thoroughly until the batter is smooth. Set aside for at least 30 minutes before using. (While the crepe batter is standing, make the filling.)

2 To make the Filling: Heat the oil in a pan. Add the onion and stir over low heat until soft. Increase the heat, add the mince and brown well. Stir in the garlic, chilli powder and paprika and cook for another minute, breaking up any lumps with a fork. Add the tomatoes, stock, lentils, sugar and wine vinegar. Cover and simmer for about 30 minutes. The lentils will absorb the liquid giving the filling a thick consistency. If it looks too dry at any stage, add a little water. Season, to taste, with salt and pepper.

3 Preheat the oven to moderate 180°C (350°F/Gas 4). Lightly brush a shallow baking dish with melted butter or oil.

4 Heat a non-stick frying pan over high heat and brush with a little oil. Pour in about 2–3 tablespoons of crepe batter and swirl it around until the entire base of the pan is covered. Cook until the underside of the crepe is golden and then flip it over with an egg slice and cook the other side. Slide it out of the pan onto a plate. Cook the rest of the crepes, greasing the pan when necessary.

5 Use 8 of the crepes. Roughly divide the filling into 8 portions and spoon a portion of the filling along the middle of each crepe. Roll up and carefully place in the dish. Sprinkle the crepes with the grated cheese and a dash of paprika. Bake for 20 minutes.

COOK'S FILE

Note: The mixture for the crepes makes about 16. For this recipe, you need only 8 crepes, but it is a good idea to make extra. You can freeze the leftovers for up to a month by stacking them between sheets of plastic wrap or greaseproof paper and sealing them in an airtight container. When you want to use them, defrost at room temperature and then reheat in the oven or microwave. They are delicious with squeezed lemon juice and sugar, maple syrup and ice cream or spread with guacamole.

Gradually add the combined egg mixture, whisking until smooth.

Cook the crepe until the underside is golden and then carefully flip it over.

Stir in the crushed garlic, chilli powder and paprika.

Add salt and pepper, to taste, to the filling after cooking.

Place one portion of the filling along the centre of each crepe.

Carefully roll up the crepe and place in the dish.

33

COTTAGE PIE

Preparation time: 30 minutes
Total cooking time: 50 minutes
Serves 4

30 g (1 oz) butter
1 kg (2 lb) finely chopped lean
    beef or lean beef mince
1 large onion, chopped
1 large carrot, diced
1/2 cup (140 g/4²/3 oz) tomato
    sauce
425 g (13¹/2 oz) can chopped
    tomatoes
1/4 cup (60 ml/2 fl oz) beef or
    vegetable stock
3/4 cup (115 g/3³/4 oz) peas
3 large potatoes, chopped
30 g (1 oz) butter
1–2 tablespoons milk

1 Heat a little oil and half the butter in a frying pan. Add the meat, in batches, and stir constantly until browned, breaking up any lumps with a fork or wooden spoon. Transfer to a bowl and set aside.

2 Add the remaining butter and a little extra oil to the pan. Stir in the onion and carrot and cook over medium heat for 3–4 minutes, or until lightly browned. Return the meat to the pan. Stir in the tomato sauce, tomatoes and stock and mix well. Reduce the heat and simmer for 10–15 minutes, or until the liquid has reduced and mixture thickened. Stir in the peas and cook for 2 minutes. Remove from the heat.

3 Add the potatoes to a large pan of water. Bring to the boil, reduce the heat and cook for 5–10 minutes, or until soft. Drain, add the butter, milk and some salt and pepper and mash until smooth and creamy.

4 Preheat the oven to moderate 180°C (350°F/Gas 4). Spoon the beef and vegetable mixture into an ovenproof dish and spread the mashed potato over the top. Place the dish on top of a baking tray and bake for 20 minutes, or until the potato topping is golden brown.

COOK'S FILE

Note: If using a cut of beef rather than mince, chop it finely with a large knife or cut it into small pieces and process in short bursts in the food processor. Rump, sirloin or fillet steak is suitable. You can use leftover cooked vegetables in the pie.

Finely chop the lean beef with a large knife or cleaver to mince it.

Stir in the tomato sauce, chopped tomatoes and stock.

Add butter and milk to the potatoes and mash until smooth and creamy.

HERB AND ONION BURGER

Preparation time: 35 minutes
Total cooking time: 10–15 minutes
Serves 4

400 g (12²/₃ oz) lean beef mince
350 g (11¼ oz) pork and veal
    mince
1 tablespoon barbecue sauce
1 small red onion, finely
    chopped
3 teaspoons chopped fresh
    parsley

3 teaspoons chopped fresh
    oregano
3 teaspoons chopped chives
1 tablespoon chopped fresh mint
30 g (1 oz) butter
6 large bulb spring onions,
    sliced into rings
4 long crusty rolls, halved and
    lightly toasted
125 g (4 oz) Camembert cheese,
    thinly sliced

1 Combine the minces, barbecue sauce, onion, herbs and some salt and pepper in a large bowl, mixing well with your hands. Divide the mixture into 4 portions and shape them into long patties.

2 Heat a frying pan or grillplate and brush liberally with oil. Cook the patties in batches for 3–4 minutes each side, or until browned and cooked through. When they are almost cooked, heat the butter in a pan, add the spring onion and cook over medium heat until wilted.

3 Place the bases of the bread rolls on serving plates. Top each with a meat patty, cheese slices, spring onion and a few oregano sprigs. Cover with the roll tops and serve with your favourite sauce or relish.

Cut the spring onion bulbs into thin rings, discarding the green tops.

Combine the minces, salt, pepper, barbecue sauce, onion and herbs.

Cook the prepared patties in batches until browned and cooked through.

SPICY CHICKEN AND BEANS

Preparation time: 30 minutes
Total cooking time: 45–50 minutes
Serves 4

1 tablespoon olive oil
4 spring onions, finely chopped
1 celery stick, finely chopped
1 jalapeño chilli, seeded and
    chopped
500 g (1 lb) chicken mince
3 cloves garlic, crushed
1/4 teaspoon ground cinnamon

1/4 teaspoon chilli powder
1 teaspoon ground cumin
2 teaspoons plain flour
425 g (13 1/2 oz) can tomatoes,
    chopped
1/2 cup (125 ml/4 fl oz) chicken
    stock
2 x 300 g (9 2/3 oz) cans large or
    small butter beans, drained
2 teaspoons soft brown sugar
3 tablespoons finely chopped
    fresh coriander

1 Heat the oil in a large frying pan, add the spring onion and cook until softened. Add the celery and chilli and cook for 1–2 minutes. Increase the heat, add the mince and brown, breaking up lumps with a fork or wooden spoon. Stir in the crushed garlic, cinnamon, chilli powder and cumin; cook for 1 minute. Add the flour to the pan and stir well.

2 Stir in the chopped tomato and stock. Bring the mixture to the boil, reduce the heat and simmer, covered, for 10–15 minutes.

3 Add the butter beans to the pan and simmer for another 15 minutes, or until the liquid is reduced to a thick sauce. Add the sugar and season, to taste. Just before serving, scatter the coriander over the top.

Add the mince to the pan and stir until brown, breaking up any lumps.

Add the tomato and chicken stock to the pan and bring to the boil.

Add the drained butter beans to the pan and simmer for another 15 minutes.

BASIL AND COCONUT CHICKEN

Preparation time: 30 minutes
Total cooking time: 15–20 minutes
Serves 4

1 tablespoon peanut oil
1 red onion, finely chopped
1 teaspoon finely chopped
    fresh red chilli
1 teaspoon finely chopped
    fresh green chilli

2 cloves garlic, crushed
1 teaspoon chopped lemon
    grass, white part only
1 teaspoon grated fresh
    ginger
500 g (1 lb) chicken mince
2 tablespoons fish sauce
1 tablespoon palm sugar or
    soft brown sugar
1 cup (250 g/8 oz) coconut
    cream
1/3 cup (20 g/2/3 oz) shredded
    fresh basil leaves
fresh red chilli, to garnish

1 Heat the oil in a frying pan, add the onion and cook over low heat for 2 minutes, or until soft. Add the red and green chilli, garlic, lemon grass and ginger and cook for 1 minute.

2 Stir in the chicken mince, breaking up any large lumps of meat with a fork or wooden spoon, then add the fish sauce and sugar.

3 Pour in the coconut cream and gently cook, without boiling, for about 10 minutes. Just before serving, stir in the basil, garnish with some red chilli and serve with jasmine rice.

Add the chillies, garlic, lemon grass and ginger to the softened onion.

Add the fish sauce and sugar to the pan and stir to combine.

Pour in the coconut cream and cook, without boiling, for about 10 minutes.

Spicy Chicken and Beans (top) with Basil and Coconut Chicken

AROUND THE WORLD

CHILLI CON CARNE

Preparation time: 15 minutes
Total cooking time: 55 minutes
Serves 4

1 tablespoon olive oil
1 onion, chopped
3 cloves garlic, crushed
1 celery stick, sliced
500 g (1 lb) lean beef mince
2 teaspoons chilli powder
pinch of cayenne pepper
1 teaspoon dried oregano
425 g (13¹/₂ oz) can crushed
    tomatoes
2 tablespoons tomato paste
1 teaspoon soft brown sugar
1 tablespoon cider vinegar or
    red wine vinegar
420 g (13¹/₃ oz) can red
    kidney beans, rinsed and
    drained

1 Heat the oil in a large, heavy-based frying pan. Add the onion, garlic and celery and stir for 5 minutes, or until softened. Add the beef mince and stir over high heat for 5 minutes, or until well browned, breaking up any lumps with a fork or wooden spoon.

2 Add the chilli powder, cayenne pepper and oregano to the frying pan. Stir well and cook over medium heat for another 5 minutes. Add the tomatoes, ¹/₂ cup (125 ml/4 fl oz) water and the tomato paste and stir well. Simmer for 30 minutes, stirring occasionally.

3 Add the sugar, vinegar, drained beans and some salt and freshly ground black pepper to the pan and cook for 5 minutes. Serve hot with white or brown rice.

COOK'S FILE

Storage time: Can be stored, covered and refrigerated, for up to 3 days.

Hint: Add more or less chilli powder, to taste. For a spicier dish, add some chopped fresh red chillies when you are cooking the onions.

Variation: If you prefer, you can use dried kidney beans in place of the canned variety. Place 250 g (8 oz) dried kidney beans in a large bowl and fill with water. Leave to soak overnight. Drain and place in a large pan, cover with water and cook for 35 minutes, or until just tender. Add the beans to the chilli at the same time as you would add the canned beans.

Add the chilli powder, cayenne and dried oregano to the meat and stir well.

Stir in the crushed tomatoes, water and tomato paste.

LARB
(Spicy Pork Salad)

Preparation time: 20 minutes
Total cooking time: 8 minutes
Serves 4–6

1 tablespoon oil
2 stems lemon grass, white part only, thinly sliced
2 fresh green chillies, finely chopped
500 g (1 lb) lean pork or beef mince
¼ cup (60 ml/2 fl oz) lime juice
2 teaspoons finely grated lime rind
2–6 teaspoons chilli sauce
lettuce leaves, for serving
⅓ cup (10 g/⅓ oz) fresh coriander leaves
¼ cup (5 g/¼ oz) small fresh mint leaves
1 small onion, very finely sliced
⅓ cup (50 g/1⅔ oz) roasted peanuts, chopped
3 tablespoons crisp fried garlic

1 Heat the oil in a wok or frying pan. Add the lemon grass, chilli and pork or beef mince. Stir-fry, breaking up any lumps of mince with a fork or wooden spoon, over high heat for 6 minutes, or until cooked through. Transfer to a bowl and allow to cool.
2 Add the lime juice and rind and the chilli sauce to the cooled mince mixture. Arrange the lettuce leaves on a serving plate. Stir most of the coriander and mint leaves, onion, peanuts and fried garlic through the mince mixture. Spoon over the lettuce and sprinkle the rest of the leaves, onion, peanuts and garlic over the top.

COOK'S FILE

Note: This is a traditional Thai dish. Crisp fried garlic is available from Asian food stores or you can make your own by finely slicing garlic and cooking over low heat in oil, stirring regularly, until crisp and golden. Drain well and cool before adding salt.

Finely slice the white part of the lemon grass with a sharp knife.

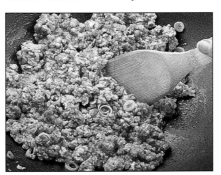

Stir-fry the lemon grass, chilli and mince, breaking up the mince as it cooks.

Add the lime juice and rind with the chilli sauce to the cooled mince.

WON TON SOUP

Preparation time: 15 minutes
+ 30 minutes soaking
Total cooking time: 20 minutes
Serves 6

3 dried Chinese mushrooms
125 g (4 oz) pork mince
60 g (2 oz) raw prawn meat,
    finely chopped
1/2 teaspoon salt
2 teaspoons soy sauce

1 teaspoon sesame oil
1 spring onion, finely chopped
1 teaspoon grated fresh ginger
1 tablespoon finely chopped
    water chestnuts
24 won ton wrappers
1.25 litres chicken stock
4 spring onions, very finely
    sliced, to garnish

1 Soak the mushrooms in hot water for 30 minutes. Drain, then squeeze out the excess moisture. Remove the stems, chop the caps finely and mix with the pork mince, prawn meat, salt, soy sauce, oil, spring onion, ginger and water chestnuts.

2 Work with 1 won ton wrapper at a time, keeping the rest covered with a tea towel. Place 1 teaspoon of the mixture on each wrapper, then moisten the edges and bring the sides up to form a pouch.

3 Cook, in batches, in a pan of boiling water for 4–5 minutes. Remove and drain. Boil the stock in a pan. Place the won tons in bowls, garnish with spring onion and pour over the stock.

Remove the stems from the moist mushrooms and chop the caps.

Measure 1 teaspoon of the mixture onto each won ton wrapper.

Fold the wrapper up around the filling, to form a pouch.

RED CURRY BEEF BALLS

Preparation time: 40 minutes
Total cooking time: 25 minutes
Serves 4

600 g (1¼ lb) lean beef mince
2 cloves garlic, crushed
3 tablespoons chopped fresh
   coriander
¼ cup (60 ml/2 fl oz) peanut oil
2 tablespoons red curry paste
1¾ cups (440 ml/14 fl oz)
   coconut milk
2 tablespoons fish sauce

3–4 teaspoons grated palm
   sugar or soft brown sugar
¼ cup (35 g/1¼ oz) ground raw
   peanuts
lime juice, to taste
chopped fresh basil, to garnish
chopped fresh mint, to garnish

1 Using your hands, combine the beef mince, garlic, coriander and some salt and pepper in a bowl. Wet your hands and shape portions of the mixture into walnut-sized balls.
2 Heat the oil in a large frying pan or wok. Cook the meatballs over medium heat, in batches, until browned.

Remove from the pan and drain on paper towels.
3 Add the curry paste to the pan and cook for 1 minute. Stir in the coconut milk, fish sauce, sugar and peanuts. Return the meatballs to the pan and simmer gently for 5–10 minutes. Squeeze lime juice, to taste, over the top and serve the meatballs sprinkled with basil and mint.

COOK'S FILE

Note: Curry pastes are available from some supermarkets and speciality Asian food stores.

Use your hands to combine the mince, garlic and coriander.

Cook the meatballs in batches, turning to brown all over.

Stir in the coconut milk, fish sauce, sugar and peanuts.

STUFFED CABBAGE ROLLS

Preparation time: 40 minutes
Total cooking time: 2 hours
Serves 4

1 large savoy cabbage
2 tablespoons olive oil
1 onion, finely chopped
2–3 cloves garlic
250 g (8 oz) pork and veal mince
150 g (4³/4 oz) ham, chopped
¹/2 cup (110 g/3²/3 oz) short-grain rice
¹/2 cup (30 g/1 oz) chopped fresh parsley
2 tablespoons chopped capers
1 tablespoon malt vinegar
1 tablespoon soft brown sugar
1 teaspoon ground allspice

Tomato Sauce
1 tablespoon olive oil
1 small onion, finely chopped
425 g (13¹/2 oz) can crushed tomatoes
3 tablespoons tomato paste
¹/2 cup (125 ml/4 fl oz) red wine
2–3 teaspoons chopped fresh thyme leaves
1 teaspoon caster sugar
30 g (1 oz) butter, cubed

1 Preheat the oven to warm 160°C (315°F/Gas 2–3). Lightly brush a 30 x 20 x 8 cm (12 x 8 x 3 inch) ovenproof dish with melted butter. Cut a circle about 5 cm (2 inches) deep around the core end of the cabbage. Carefully remove 8 outer cabbage leaves (discard the inside of the cabbage, or use for coleslaw). Plunge the whole leaves, in batches, in a large pan of boiling, salted water for 2 minutes, or until just wilted. Drain.
2 Heat the oil in a pan and cook the onion and garlic for 2–3 minutes, or until soft. Add the mince and cook for 2–3 minutes, breaking up any lumps with a fork or wooden spoon. Add the ham and rice, stir for 2 minutes, then transfer to a bowl and add the parsley, capers, vinegar, sugar and allspice.
3 Divide the mixture into 8 portions. Cut away the hard centre of each cabbage leaf. Then overlap pieces of leaf where the hard stem has been removed. Place a portion of filling on each leaf, fold in the sides and roll into a parcel, about 12 cm (5 inches) long. Arrange rolls, seam-side-down, close together in the dish. Try not to leave any gaps between the rolls.
4 To make Tomato Sauce: Heat the oil in a pan and cook the onion for 2–3 minutes. Stir in the tomatoes, tomato paste, wine, thyme and sugar and cook for another 10 minutes. Pour the sauce over the rolls.
5 Dot with butter, cover the dish tightly with a lid or foil and bake for 1¹/2 hours, or until tender.

Use a small, sharp knife to cut out the core of the cabbage.

Roll each filled leaf into a parcel, completely enclosing the filling.

Stir in the tomatoes, tomato paste, wine, thyme and sugar.

MOUSSAKA

Preparation time: 20 minutes
  + 1 hour standing
Total cooking time: 1 hour 45 minutes
Serves 6

3 medium eggplants
1/2 cup (125 ml/4 fl oz) olive oil

Mince Sauce
2 tablespoons olive oil
1 large onion, finely chopped
500 g (1 lb) lean beef mince
2 tablespoons dry white wine
425 g (13 1/2 oz) can tomato purée
1 tablespoon finely chopped
    fresh flat-leaf parsley
2 teaspoons finely chopped
    fresh mint leaves
1/2 teaspoon ground cinnamon

Cheese Sauce
90 g (3 oz) butter
1/3 cup (40 g/1 1/3 oz) plain flour
2 cups (500 ml/16 fl oz) milk
2 eggs, lightly beaten
2/3 cup (85 g/2 3/4 oz) freshly
    grated Romano cheese

1 Cut the unpeeled eggplants into 1 cm (1/2 inch) slices. Sprinkle both sides with salt and leave in a colander for 1 hour. Rinse under cold water, then drain well. Squeeze out any excess moisture with paper towels.
2 To make Mince Sauce: Heat the oil in a pan. Add the onion and mince and stir over high heat for 10 minutes, or until the meat is well browned and all the liquid has evaporated. Add the wine, tomato purée, herbs, cinnamon and some white pepper and bring to the boil. Reduce heat and simmer, covered, for 20 minutes, stirring occasionally. Remove the lid and simmer for 10 minutes.

3 To make Cheese Sauce: Heat the butter in a small pan until foaming and then stir in the flour over low heat for 2 minutes. Add the milk gradually, stirring until smooth. Stir over medium heat for 5 minutes, or until the mixture boils and thickens. Cook for 1 minute, then remove from the heat. Add the eggs and cheese and beat until smooth.

4 Preheat the oven to moderate 180°C (350°F/Gas 4). Heat the oil in a heavy-based pan and cook the eggplant slices, a few at a time, until golden. Remove and drain on paper towels. Place a third of the eggplant in a shallow ovenproof dish. Cover with half the Mince Sauce, a layer of eggplant, and then another layer of each. Spread Cheese Sauce over the top layer of eggplant. Bake for 45 minutes, or until golden. Leave in the dish for 5 minutes before serving.

Sprinkle both sides of the eggplant slices with salt.

Stir the meat over high heat until all the liquid has evaporated.

Add the lightly beaten eggs and cheese and beat until smooth.

SPICY LAMB TRIANGLES

Preparation time: 40 minutes
Total cooking time: 20 minutes
Makes 15

1 onion, finely chopped
400 g (12²/₃ oz) lamb mince
1 clove garlic, crushed
¹/₂ teaspoon cumin seeds
¹/₂ teaspoon ground cumin
1 teaspoon chilli powder
3 tablespoons pine nuts
1 tablespoon chopped fresh mint
3 tablespoons chopped fresh
   coriander
1 tablespoon mango chutney

1 egg, lightly beaten
10 sheets filo pastry
75 g (2¹/₂ oz) butter, melted

1 Heat a little olive oil in a frying pan, add the onion and lamb mince and brown. Mix in the garlic, cumin seeds, ground cumin and chilli and stir for 1 minute. Add the pine nuts, mint, coriander, chutney and egg and mix well. Season, to taste, with salt and pepper. Preheat the oven to moderately hot 200°C (400°F/Gas 6).
2 Cover the filo pastry with a damp tea towel and work with 1 sheet at a time to prevent it drying out. Brush a sheet with melted butter. Lay a second sheet on top, brush with butter and

then cut lengthways into 3 pieces. Place a tablespoon of mixture onto the end of each. Roll up into triangles by folding one corner end of the pastry over, forming a triangle. Continue rolling until you reach the end of the strip. Repeat this with the other 2 strips of filo and then repeat with the remaining filo and filling.
3 Line a baking tray with baking paper, place the triangles on the tray and brush the tops with melted butter. Bake for 12 minutes, or until golden.

C O O K ' S   F I L E

Storage time: Cooked triangles can be frozen on an oven tray until firm, then placed in an airtight container.

Add the egg to the onion and meat mixture and stir thoroughly.

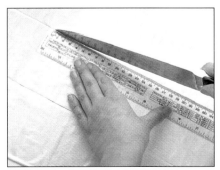

Using a ruler as a guide, cut the filo pastry into 3, lengthways.

Continue rolling each triangle to the end of the strip of filo.

EMPANADAS

Preparation time: 40 minutes
 + 30 minutes standing
Total cooking time: 40 minutes
Makes 10

1 tablespoon oil
4 rashers bacon, chopped
1 large onion, finely chopped
3 cloves garlic, chopped
150 g (4¾ oz) pork and veal mince
150 g (4¾ oz) chicken mince
2 tablespoons tomato paste
1 teaspoon soft brown sugar
2 hard-boiled eggs, chopped
4 gherkins, finely chopped
½ cup (25 g/¾ oz) chopped fresh coriander leaves
1 egg white, beaten
oil, for shallow-frying

Pastry
2¼ cups (280 g/9 oz) plain flour
½ cup (125 ml/4 fl oz) water
1 egg, beaten
1 teaspoon caster sugar
50 g (1⅔ oz) butter, melted, plus some for brushing

1 Heat the oil in a pan. Add the bacon, onion and garlic and cook over medium heat for 5 minutes, stirring regularly. Add the pork and veal and chicken mince and cook for another 5 minutes, or until well browned, breaking up any lumps with a fork or wooden spoon.

2 Add the tomato paste, sugar and 1 tablespoon of water to the pan and bring to the boil, stirring constantly. Reduce the heat and simmer for 20 minutes. Stir in the egg, gherkin and chopped coriander. Remove from the heat and set aside for at least 30 minutes to cool.

3 To make Pastry: Process the flour, water, egg, sugar and butter in a food processor for 20–30 seconds, or until the mixture comes together. Turn out onto a lightly floured surface and gather the pastry together into a ball. Cover with plastic wrap and set aside for 10 minutes.

4 Roll the pastry out to a 30 x 20 cm (12 x 8 inch) rectangle. Brush with melted butter and tightly roll the pastry up into a sausage. Cut into 3 cm (1¼ inch) slices and cover with a clean tea towel to prevent the pastry drying out.

5 Roll out 1 slice of pastry to form a 12 cm (5 inch) circle. In the centre, place 2 tablespoons of the filling and lightly brush the edges with egg white. Bring 1 side over to meet the other. Press the edges to seal and use a fork to decorate the edge. Place the filled pastry on a baking tray and repeat with the remaining filling and pastry slices.

6 Heat 2 cm (¾ inch) oil in a large pan, add the pastries and cook, in batches, for 2–3 minutes each side over medium heat. Drain on paper towels and serve.

COOK'S FILE

Variation: Empanadas are Spanish specialities, which vary greatly in size. These little ones make great snacks, but you can also make larger ones for a delicious lunch. To make them, cut the pastry roll into 5 cm (2 inch) slices. Then roll the circles of pastry into 16 cm (6½ inch) rounds. Double the amount of filling in the centre, fold the pastry over and seal the edge. When cooking, add a little extra oil to the pan and extend the cooking time.

Add the pork and veal and chicken mince and cook for another 5 minutes.

Stir in the egg, gherkin and chopped fresh coriander.

Process the pastry ingredients in a food processor until they come together.

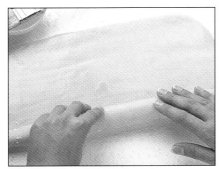

Tightly roll up the pastry into a sausage shape before slicing.

Spoon 2 tablespoons of the filling onto the centre of each circle of pastry.

Brush pastry edges with egg white and bring one side over to meet the other.

SAN CHOY BAU

Preparation time: 20 minutes
Total cooking time: 10 minutes
Serves 2–4

1 tablespoon peanut oil
1 teaspoon sesame oil
1–2 cloves garlic, crushed
1 tablespoon grated fresh ginger
4 spring onions, chopped
500 g (1 lb) lean pork mince
1 red capsicum, seeded and
    finely diced
230 g (7⅓ oz) can water
    chestnuts, drained and
    roughly chopped
1–2 tablespoons soy sauce
1 tablespoon oyster sauce
2 tablespoons dry sherry
1 iceberg or butter lettuce

1 Heat the oils in a large, non-stick frying pan or wok. Add the garlic, ginger and spring onion and stir for about 2 minutes. Add the pork mince and cook over medium heat until well browned, breaking up any lumps with a fork or wooden spoon.
2 Stir in the capsicum, chestnuts, soy and oyster sauces and sherry. Simmer over medium heat until the liquid reduces and thickens. Keep warm.
3 Wash the lettuce and separate the whole leaves. Shake off the excess water. Place the lettuce cups on a plate and spoon in some pork mixture.

COOK'S FILE

Note: You can also serve the lettuce leaves and pork mixture separately. Let everybody fill their own lettuce leaf with the pork, wrapping the lettuce around to form a package to hold with their fingers.

Drain the can of water chestnuts and roughly chop them.

Add the garlic, ginger and spring onion to the wok and stir for about 2 minutes.

Stir in the capsicum, water chestnuts, soy and oyster sauces and sherry.

MEXICAN BEEF AND JALAPENO PIZZA

Preparation time: 30 minutes
Total cooking time: 45 minutes
Makes 2 large pizzas

2 tablespoons olive oil
1 onion, finely chopped
1 green capsicum, finely diced
1 teaspoon chilli paste
2 cloves garlic, crushed
500 g (1 lb) lean beef mince
1/2 teaspoon ground cinnamon
1/2 teaspoon cayenne pepper
1/4 teaspoon ground cloves

1 tablespoon balsamic vinegar
425 g (13 1/2 oz) can crushed
  tomatoes
1/2 cup (125 g/4 oz) tomato paste
2 bay leaves
3 tablespoons sliced jalapeño
  chillies
2 x 30 cm (12 inch) ready-made
  pizza bases
150 g (4 3/4 oz) Cheddar cheese,
  grated
100 g (3 1/3 oz) corn chips

1 Heat 1 tablespoon of the oil in a large pan. Add the onion, capsicum, chilli paste and garlic and stir-fry for 2–3 minutes. Add the beef mince and brown for 4–5 minutes.

2 Add the spices, vinegar, tomatoes, tomato paste, bay leaves and chillies, mix well, reduce the heat and simmer for 8–10 minutes. Remove from the heat and allow to cool slightly. Discard the bay leaves. Preheat the oven to moderately hot 200°C (400°F/Gas 6).

3 Spoon the beef mixture onto the pizza bases, leaving a 2 cm (3/4 inch) border around the edge. Brush the edges with extra olive oil. Sprinkle the top with cheese and tuck corn chips into the meat mixture. Transfer to an oven tray and bake for 20–25 minutes, or until the cheese is golden.

Add the beef mince to the onion mixture in the pan.

Add the spices, vinegar, tomatoes, tomato paste, bay leaves and chillies to the pan.

Sprinkle grated Cheddar cheese over the top of the pizza.

VIETNAMESE PORK AND PRAWN SPRING ROLLS

Preparation time: 40 minutes
Total cooking time: 10 minutes
Serves 4–6

8–12 large sheets dried rice paper
1 tablespoon peanut oil
1 stem lemon grass, white part only, chopped
2 cloves garlic, finely chopped
500 g (1 lb) pork mince
500 g (1 lb) raw prawns, shelled and deveined
2 tablespoons fish sauce
1 tablespoon soy sauce
1 tablespoon sweet chilli sauce
1 tablespoon toasted sesame seeds
8 butter lettuce leaves, washed, dried and chilled
1 Lebanese cucumber, cut into matchsticks
1 large carrot, finely grated
1/2 cup (10 g/1/3 oz) fresh small mint leaves (or large chopped leaves)
4 tablespoons finely chopped roasted peanuts

Dipping Sauce
2 cloves garlic, crushed
1 tablespoon minced fresh red chilli
1 tablespoon white sugar
2 tablespoons soy sauce
1 tablespoon fish sauce
1 tablespoon rice wine vinegar
1 tablespoon crunchy peanut butter
1 tablespoon finely chopped fresh coriander

1 Brush each rice paper sheet on both sides with some water and spread out on damp tea towels. Cover with more damp towels and leave until softened.

2 Heat the peanut oil in a pan, add the lemon grass and garlic and fry for 1 minute. Add the pork mince and prawns and stir for 3–4 minutes, or until they change colour. Stir in the sauces and sesame seeds and simmer for 4–5 minutes.

3 Place a lettuce leaf on a rice paper sheet, top with the pork and prawn mixture, cucumber, carrot, mint and nuts, fold in the sides and roll up. Repeat with the remaining rice paper sheets and ingredients.

4 To make Dipping Sauce: Mix all the ingredients in a small bowl. Serve with the spring rolls.

Cut the Lebanese cucumber into fine matchsticks, using a sharp knife.

Use a pastry brush to moisten each rice paper sheet with water.

Fold in the sides of the sheet and roll up into a parcel.

THAI FISH CAKES

Preparation time: 25 minutes
Total cooking time: 10 minutes
Serves 4–6

450 g (14¹/₃ oz) firm white
    fish fillets
3 tablespoons cornflour
1 tablespoon fish sauce
1 egg, beaten
¹/₂ cup (15 g/¹/₂ oz) fresh
    coriander leaves
1–2 teaspoons chopped red
    chilli, optional

3 teaspoons red curry paste
100 g (3¹/₃ oz) green beans,
    very finely sliced
2 spring onions, finely chopped
¹/₂ cup (125 ml/4 fl oz) oil
sweet chilli sauce, to serve

1 Process the fish in a food processor for 20 seconds, or until smooth. Add the cornflour, fish sauce, beaten egg, coriander leaves, red chilli and curry paste. Process for 10 seconds, or until well combined.
2 Transfer the fish mixture to a large bowl. Add the beans and spring onion and mix well. Using wet hands, form

2 tablespoons of the mixture at a time into flattish patties.
3 Heat the oil in a heavy-based frying pan over medium heat. Cook 4 fish cakes at a time until golden brown on both sides. Drain on paper towels and serve immediately with some sweet chilli sauce.

COOK'S FILE

Storage time: You can prepare the fish cakes up to 4 hours in advance. After forming into patties, cover them lightly with plastic wrap and store in the refrigerator until you are ready to use them.

Add the cornflour, fish sauce, egg, coriander, paste and chilli.

Form 2 rounded tablespoons of the mixture at a time into flattish patties.

Cook the fish cakes in oil, until golden on both sides.

LASAGNE

Preparation time: 40 minutes
Total cooking time: 1 hour 40 minutes
Serves 6–8

2 tablespoons oil
30 g (1 oz) butter
1 large onion, finely chopped
1 carrot, finely chopped
1 celery stick, finely chopped
500 g (1 lb) lean beef mince
150 g (4³/4 oz) chicken livers,
    finely chopped
1 cup (250 g/8 oz) tomato purée
1 cup (250 ml/8 fl oz) red
    wine
2 tablespoons chopped fresh
    parsley
375 g (12 oz) fresh lasagne
    sheets
1 cup (100 g/3¹/3 oz) freshly
    grated Parmesan

Béchamel Sauce
60 g (2 oz) butter
¹/3 cup (40 g/1¹/3 oz) flour
2¹/4 cups (560 ml/18 fl oz) milk
¹/2 teaspoon nutmeg

1 Heat the oil and butter in a heavy-based pan. Add the onion, carrot and celery and stir constantly over medium heat until softened. Increase the heat, add the beef mince and brown well, breaking up any lumps with a fork or wooden spoon.
2 Add the chicken liver and cook until it changes colour. Mix in the tomato purée, red wine, parsley and some salt and freshly ground black pepper, to taste. Bring the mixture to the boil, reduce the heat and simmer for 45 minutes. Remove from the heat and set aside.

3 **To make Béchamel Sauce:** Melt the butter in a pan over low heat until foaming, add the flour and stir constantly for 2 minutes. Remove the pan from the heat and gradually stir in the milk. Return to the heat and bring to the boil, stirring constantly until thickened. When thick, reduce heat and simmer for 2 minutes. Season well with nutmeg and salt and pepper. Place a piece of plastic wrap on the surface of the sauce to prevent a skin forming and set aside.
4 Cut the lasagne sheets so they will fit snugly into a deep, rectangular ovenproof dish. Some fresh lasagne sheets require precooking by plunging in boiling water for 1–2 minutes to soften, so follow the manufacturer's instructions. If you are precooking the lasagne sheets, drain them well on a tea towel.
5 Preheat the oven to moderate 180°C (350°F/Gas 4). Brush an ovenproof dish with melted butter. Spread a thin layer of the meat sauce over the base and top with a thin layer of Béchamel. If Béchamel has cooled and become too thick, warm it gently to make spreading easier. Lay lasagne sheets on top, gently pressing to push out any air.
6 Continue the layers, finishing with the Béchamel. Sprinkle with Parmesan and bake for 35–40 minutes, or until the top is golden. Let the lasagne stand for 15 minutes before serving, to make cutting easier.

COOK'S FILE

Note: A 375 g (12 oz) packet of instant lasagne can be used instead of fresh lasagne. Follow the manufacturer's instructions—usually the sheets can be used without any precooking.

Add the onion, carrot and celery to the pan and stir until softened.

Add the chicken liver to the mixture and cook until it changes colour.

Season the Béchamel Sauce with salt, pepper and nutmeg.

When the sauce is cooked, place a piece of plastic wrap on the surface.

Cut the lasagne sheets so that they fit snugly in the ovenproof dish.

Spread a thin layer of the meat sauce over the base of the dish.

BAKED CANNELLONI MILANESE

Preparation time: 20 minutes
Total cooking time: 1 hour 40 minutes
Serves 4

500 g (1 lb) pork and veal
    mince
2/3 cup (55 g/1³/4 oz) fresh
    breadcrumbs
1 cup (100 g/3¹/3 oz) freshly
    grated Parmesan
2 eggs, beaten
1 tablespoon chopped fresh
    oregano
12–15 cannelloni tubes
375 g (12 oz) fresh ricotta
    cheese
1/2 cup (60 g/2 oz) freshly
    grated Cheddar cheese

Tomato Sauce
425 g (13¹/2 oz) can
    tomato purée
425 g (13¹/2 oz) can chopped
    tomatoes
2 cloves garlic, crushed
1/4 cup (15 g/¹/2 oz) chopped
    fresh basil

1 Preheat the oven to moderate 180°C (350°F/Gas 4). Brush an ovenproof dish with a little oil or melted butter.
2 In a bowl, combine the pork and veal mince, breadcrumbs, half the Parmesan, the beaten eggs, oregano and some salt and freshly ground black pepper. Use your fingers to stuff the mince mixture into the cannelloni tubes. Set aside.
3 To make Tomato Sauce: Combine the tomato purée, chopped tomatoes and garlic in a pan and bring to the boil. Reduce the heat and simmer for 15 minutes. Add the chopped basil, season with freshly ground pepper and stir well.
4 Spoon half the Tomato Sauce over the base of the prepared dish. Arrange the stuffed cannelloni tubes on top. Cover with the remaining sauce. Spread with ricotta cheese.
5 Sprinkle the remaining Parmesan and the Cheddar over the top. Bake, covered with foil, for 1 hour. Remove the foil and bake for another 15 minutes, or until golden. Let it stand for 5 minutes before serving.

Combine the mince with the other ingredients until thoroughly mixed.

Use your fingers to push the mince mixture into the cannelloni tubes.

Add the chopped basil to the tomato mixture and season with pepper.

Arrange the stuffed cannelloni tubes on top of the sauce.

SPRING ROLLS

Preparation time: 40 minutes
Total cooking time: 20–25 minutes
Makes 18

2 tablespoons oil
2 cloves garlic, chopped
3 cm (1¼ inch) piece of fresh
 ginger, grated
100 g (3⅓ oz) lean pork mince
100 g (3⅓ oz) chicken mince
50 g (1⅔ oz) raw prawns, minced
2 celery sticks, finely sliced
1 small carrot, finely chopped
½ cup (90 g/3 oz) chopped
 water chestnuts
4 spring onions, chopped
1 cup (75 g/2½ oz) finely
 shredded cabbage
½ cup (125 ml/4 fl oz) chicken
 stock
4 tablespoons cornflour
2 tablespoons oyster sauce
1 tablespoon soy sauce
2 teaspoons sesame oil
⅓ cup (80 ml/2¾ fl oz) water
36 spring roll wrappers
3 cups (750 ml/24 fl oz) oil
sweet chilli sauce, for serving

1 Heat 1 tablespoon oil in a wok or pan and cook the garlic and ginger for 30 seconds. Add the pork, chicken and prawn minces and cook for 3 minutes, or until the minces are brown. Transfer to a bowl.
2 Wipe the pan, then heat the remaining tablespoon of oil and add the celery, carrot, water chestnuts, spring onion and cabbage. Stir over medium heat for 2 minutes. Combine the chicken stock, 1 tablespoon cornflour, oyster and soy sauces and salt and pepper, add to the vegetables and stir until thickened. Stir the sesame oil and vegetables into the meat mixture and cool. Mix the remaining cornflour with the water until smooth.
3 Place 1 small square spring roll wrapper on the bench with a corner towards you. Brush all the edges with a little cornflour paste and cover with another wrapper. Brush the edges of the second wrapper and spread about 1½ tablespoons of the filling across the bottom corner of the wrapper. Fold the bottom corner up over the filling, fold in the sides and roll up firmly. Repeat with the remaining wrappers and filling. Heat the oil in a deep pan and fry the rolls, in batches, for 2–3 minutes, or until golden. Drain and serve with sweet chilli sauce.

Add the pork, chicken and prawn minces to the wok or pan and fry until brown.

Mix the stock, 1 tablespoon of cornflour, oyster and soy sauces and seasoning.

Fold the bottom corner over the filling and fold in the sides before rolling up.

Sauces and Dips for Meatballs

MEATBALLS

Combine 750 g (1½ lb) lean beef mince, 1 very finely chopped onion, 1 lightly beaten egg, 2 crushed garlic cloves, 2–3 tablespoons fresh breadcrumbs and lots of salt and freshly ground black pepper in a large bowl. Use your hands to mix well. Then wet your hands and roll tablespoons of the mince mixture into balls. Heat some oil in a large frying pan and cook the meatballs in batches over medium heat, turning regularly until browned and cooked through. Serve the meatballs on skewers or toothpicks with one or two of the sauces. These meatballs can be made and cooked several hours in advance. Refrigerate until needed and then reheat in a moderate oven for 10–15 minutes. Makes about 45.

BARBECUE SAUCE

Add 1 small, chopped onion to a lightly oiled pan and cook over low heat for 3 minutes, or until soft. Add 1 tablespoon each of malt vinegar, Worcestershire sauce and soft brown sugar, plus ⅓ cup (80 ml/2¾ fl oz) tomato sauce. Bring to the boil, reduce the heat and simmer for about 3 minutes. Serve warm or at room temperature with the meatballs.

DILL SAUCE

Combine ½ cup (125 g/4 oz) each of plain yoghurt and sour cream, 1 tablespoon horseradish cream, ¼ cup (15 g/½ oz) chopped fresh dill, 2 finely chopped spring onions and some salt and pepper, to taste. Mix well and serve chilled.

CAPSICUM MAYONNAISE

Cut a large red capsicum in half, remove the seeds and membrane and brush the skin lightly with oil. Grill, skin-side-up, until the skin blisters and blackens. Cover the capsicum with a tea towel. When cool enough to handle, peel away the skin and place the flesh in a food processor. Add ¾ cup (185 g/6 oz) whole egg mayonnaise, 1–2 cloves garlic, salt, pepper and a squeeze of lemon juice. Process until smooth. You could also add some chopped fresh basil.

HERB SAUCE

Combine 200 g (6½ oz) plain yoghurt, 1 tablespoon each of chopped fresh mint, coriander and lemon thyme, 2 tablespoons cream and 1 teaspoon freshly grated ginger. You could also add 1 small peeled, seeded and finely chopped Lebanese cucumber.

CHILLI AND LIME SAUCE

Combine ¼ cup (60 ml/2 fl oz) sweet chilli sauce, 2 teaspoons soft brown sugar, 1 teaspoon finely grated lime rind, 3–4 teaspoons lime juice and 1 tablespoon freshly chopped basil.

PEANUT SAUCE

Heat 3 teaspoons peanut oil in a pan. Add 1 small, finely chopped onion and cook for 3 minutes, or until soft. Stir in 2 crushed cloves garlic, 2 teaspoons each of grated fresh ginger and ground cumin and 1 teaspoon red curry paste. Cook, stirring, for 1 minute. Stir in 1½ cups (375 ml/12 fl oz) coconut milk, ½ cup (80 g/2⅔ oz) very finely chopped peanuts and 2 tablespoons soft brown sugar. Simmer the sauce over low heat for 5 minutes, or until reduced slightly and thickened. Add a little lemon juice, to taste. Serve the sauce warm.

CORIANDER SAUCE

In a bowl, combine ¼ cup (60 ml/2 fl oz) fish sauce, 1 tablespoon white vinegar, 2–3 teaspoons finely chopped fresh red chillies, 1 teaspoon sugar and 3 teaspoons chopped fresh coriander. Add a good squeeze of lime juice, mix well and serve.

Left to right: Meatballs; Barbecue Sauce; Dill Sauce; Capsicum Mayonnaise; Herb Sauce; Chilli and Lime Sauce; Peanut Sauce; Coriander Sauce

FISH CAKES IN CORN HUSKS

Preparation time: 20 minutes
Total cooking time: 20 minutes
Serves 4

2 cobs of corn with full husks
500 g (1 lb) white fish fillets
juice and grated rind of 1 lime
1/2 teaspoon paprika
1/4 cup (30 g/1 oz) grated strong
    Cheddar cheese
1 tablespoon snipped fresh chives

Mexican Salsa
1 red onion, finely chopped
2 large tomatoes, chopped
1 fresh red chilli, finely chopped
1 tablespoon chopped fresh
    coriander
1 tablespoon lime juice

1 Preheat the oven to moderately hot 200°C (400°F/Gas 6). Carefully remove the husks and silk from the corn and discard the silk. Place 1 piece of husk on a board with the wide end away from you. Place another piece inside it, with the wide end towards you. Make 3 more and then reserve 4 pieces of husk.
2 To make Mexican Salsa: Mix all the ingredients in a bowl.
3 Cut the kernels from the cob and mix in a food processor with the fish, lime juice and rind and paprika. Transfer to a bowl and mix in the cheese and chives. Divide the mixture into 4 and spoon into the corn husks. Cover with the reserved husks and tie with a piece of string to seal. Place on a non-stick baking tray and bake for 20 minutes, or until tender. Serve with the Mexican Salsa.

Place pieces of husk inside one another. Put the wide ends on top of the pointed ends.

Use a sharp knife to cut the kernels from the corn cobs.

Spoon the fish mixture into the prepared corn husks.

BEEF AND SPINACH CURRY

Preparation time: 30 minutes
Total cooking time: 1 hour 15 minutes
Serves 4

2 tablespoons oil
1 onion, finely chopped
2 cloves garlic, finely chopped
2 teaspoons ground cumin
2 teaspoons ground coriander
2 teaspoons paprika
1 teaspoon garam masala
1 teaspoon turmeric
1/2 teaspoon finely chopped fresh red chilli

1 teaspoon finely chopped fresh green chilli
2 teaspoons grated fresh ginger
500 g (1 lb) lean beef or lamb mince
1 tomato, chopped
1 cup (250 ml/8 fl oz) beef stock or water
500 g (1 lb) English spinach, chopped
200 g (61/2 oz) plain yoghurt

1 Heat 1 tablespoon of the oil in a large pan and cook the onion over medium heat until golden brown. Add the garlic, cumin, coriander, paprika, garam masala, turmeric, red and green chilli and the grated ginger and stir for

1 minute. Remove and set aside.
2 Heat the remaining oil in the pan and brown the meat in batches over high heat, breaking up any lumps with a fork or wooden spoon. Return the onion mixture to the pan and add the tomato and stock or water.
3 Bring the mixture to the boil and then reduce the heat and simmer for about 1 hour. Season with salt, to taste. Meanwhile, cook the spinach. Just before serving, add the spinach to the mixture and stir in the yoghurt.

COOK'S FILE

Note: If possible, make the beef mixture in advance and refrigerate overnight for the flavours to develop.

Finely chop the chillies. Wear rubber gloves to prevent skin irritation.

Add the garlic, spices, red and green chilli and ginger to the pan and stir.

Add the tomato and stock or water to the pan and bring the mixture to the boil.

BAKED KIBBEH

Preparation time: 1 hour
Total cooking time: 30 minutes
Serves 8–10

1³/4 cups (310 g/9³/4 oz) fine
   burghul
olive oil or ghee
1.1 kg (2 lb 3¹/3 oz) lean lamb
   mince
2 onions, chopped
¹/2 teaspoon chilli flakes
1¹/2 teaspoons sweet paprika
¹/4 teaspoon ground cinnamon
¹/4 teaspoon ground allspice
¹/2 cup (60 g/2 oz) finely
   chopped walnuts
¹/2 cup (65 g/2¹/4 oz) finely
   chopped pistachios
¹/2 cup (30 g/1 oz) chopped
   fresh parsley
¹/4 cup (60 g/2 oz) plain yoghurt,
   well-drained (see Note)
2 ice cubes
³/4 cup (165 g/5¹/2 oz) mashed
   potato

1 Place the burghul in a sieve and rinse well under cold running water. Set aside for at least 15 minutes. Heat about 1 tablespoon of oil or ghee in a large frying pan. Add 350 g (11¹/4 oz) of the lamb mince and cook over medium heat for about 3 minutes, breaking up any lumps with a fork or wooden spoon. Add half the onion and some salt and freshly ground black pepper and cook until the mince is well browned.

2 Add the chilli flakes, 1 teaspoon sweet paprika, ground cinnamon, ground allspice, walnuts and half the pistachios and continue cooking until the mince is almost crispy. Drain away any excess fat. Allow the mixture to cool completely, then stir in the parsley and well-drained yoghurt. Set aside.

3 Process the remaining mince, onion and paprika with 1 teaspoon of ground black pepper and some salt in a food processor until the mixture is smooth. Remove half the meat mixture, add an ice cube and half the burghul to the processor and process until smooth. Remove from the processor and then repeat with the remaining meat, ice cube and burghul. Preheat the oven to moderately hot 190°C (375°F/Gas 5).

4 Transfer all the processed meat and burghul mixture to a bowl. Knead in the mashed potato until the mixture is almost like a bread dough. With wet hands, press half the mixture firmly into the base of a lightly oiled 23 x 32 x 5 cm (9 x 13 x 2 inch) baking dish, spreading it evenly.

5 Spread the cold yoghurt and mince mixture on top and gently press into the surface. Press the remaining doughy mixture evenly over the top. Score the top in a crisscross pattern, cutting at least two-thirds of the way through. Gently loosen the edges with a spatula.

6 Sprinkle the top with a little cold water and 2 tablespoons of melted ghee or oil. Scatter over the remaining pistachios. Bake for 15 minutes, then remove and baste quickly. Continue to bake for another 10 minutes. Place under a preheated grill to brown the top. Serve with some plain yoghurt.

COOK'S FILE

Note: To drain the yoghurt, place in a muslin-lined sieve for approximately 2 hours, allowing the excess liquid to drain away.

Rinse the burghul in a sieve under cold running water.

Add the chilli flakes, spices and nuts to the meat and continue cooking.

Process the remaining mince, onion, paprika, pepper and salt, until smooth.

Knead the mixture with your hands until it is almost like a bread dough.

Press the cold mince and yoghurt mixture over the top of the doughy mixture.

Use a sharp knife to score a crisscross pattern on the top.

INDIAN SEEKH KEBABS

Preparation time: 40 minutes
Total cooking time: 12 minutes
Serves 4

pinch of ground cloves
pinch of ground nutmeg
1/2 teaspoon chilli powder
1 teaspoon ground cumin
2 teaspoons ground coriander
3 cloves garlic, finely chopped
5 cm (2 inch) piece of fresh
    ginger, grated
500 g (1 lb) lean beef mince
1 tablespoon oil
2 tablespoons lemon juice

Onion and Mint Relish
1 red onion, finely chopped
1 tablespoon white vinegar
1 tablespoon lemon juice
1 tablespoon chopped fresh mint

1 Soak 12 thick wooden skewers in cold water for 15 minutes. Dry-fry the cloves, nutmeg, chilli, cumin and coriander in a heavy-based frying pan, over low heat, for about 2 minutes, shaking the pan constantly. Transfer to a bowl with the garlic and ginger and set aside.

2 Knead the mince firmly using your fingertips and the base of your hand. The meat needs to be kneaded constantly for about 3 minutes, or until it becomes very soft and a little sticky. This process changes the texture of the meat when cooked, making it very soft and tender. Add the mince to the spice and garlic mixture and mix well, seasoning with plenty of salt and pepper.

3 Form tablespoons of the meat into small, round patty shapes. Wet your hands and press 2 portions of the meat around a skewer, leaving a gap of about 3 cm (1¼ inches) at the top of the skewer. Smooth the outside gently, place on baking paper and refrigerate while making the remaining kebabs.

4 To make Onion and Mint Relish: Combine the onion, vinegar and lemon juice in a small bowl; refrigerate for 10 minutes. Stir in the mint and season with pepper, to taste, just before serving.

5 Brush a preheated grill or hotplate with the oil. Grill the skewers for about 8 minutes, turning regularly and sprinkling with a little lemon juice. Serve with steamed rice and the Onion and Mint Relish.

Use a sharp knife to finely chop the cloves of garlic.

Dry-fry the cloves, nutmeg, chilli, cumin and coriander in a heavy-based pan.

Press two rounds of meat around each wooden skewer.

COMBINATION DIM SIMS

Preparation time: 1 hour + refrigeration
Total cooking time: 30 minutes
Makes about 30

6 dried Chinese mushrooms
1 cup (250 ml/8 fl oz) hot water
200 g (6¹/2 oz) lean pork mince
30 g (1 oz) pork fat, finely
    chopped
100 g (3¹/3 oz) raw prawn meat,
    finely chopped
2 spring onions, finely chopped
1 tablespoon sliced bamboo
    shoots, finely chopped

1 celery stick, finely chopped
3 teaspoons cornflour
2 teaspoons soy sauce
1 teaspoon caster sugar
30 won ton or egg noodle
    wrappers

1 Soak the mushrooms in hot water for 10 minutes, drain and chop finely, discarding the hard stems.
2 Mix the mushrooms, pork mince, pork fat, prawn, spring onion, bamboo shoots and celery in a bowl. Combine the cornflour, soy, sugar and salt and pepper into a smooth paste in another bowl. Stir into the pork mixture, cover and refrigerate for 1 hour.

3 Work with 1 wrapper at a time, keeping the rest covered with a tea towel. Place 1 tablespoon of filling in the centre of each wrapper. Moisten the edges with water and fold the corners into the centre. Press the corners together to seal. Set aside on a lightly floured surface.
4 Line the base of a bamboo steamer with a circle of baking paper. Arrange the dim sims on the paper, spacing them well (they will need to be cooked in batches). Cover the steamer and cook over a pan of simmering water for 8 minutes, or until the wrappers are firm and the filling is cooked. Serve with chilli or soy sauce.

Soak the dried mushrooms in hot water to rehydrate them.

Fold the corners into the centre and press together to seal.

Arrange a circle of baking paper in the base of a bamboo steamer.

MIDDLE-EASTERN MINCE WITH CHICKPEAS AND EGGPLANT

Preparation time: 45 minutes
Total cooking time: 25–30 minutes
Serves 4

3 tablespoons olive oil
1 red onion, finely chopped
2 cloves garlic, finely chopped
2 teaspoons ground coriander
1 teaspoon ground cumin
500 g (1 lb) lean beef mince
1 cup (250 ml/8 fl oz) beef stock
1–2 tablespoons raisins
300 g (9²/₃ oz) can chickpeas, drained
1 large ripe tomato, seeded and chopped
1 tablespoon chopped fresh coriander
1 tablespoon chopped fresh mint
1 teaspoon turmeric
4 slender eggplants, cut in half lengthways

Yoghurt Dressing
1 cup (250 g/8 oz) thick plain yoghurt
2 tablespoons chopped fresh coriander
1 tablespoon lemon juice

1 Heat 1 tablespoon of oil in a large frying pan. Add the onion, garlic, coriander and cumin and cook for 5 minutes over medium heat. Add the mince and stir regularly until just browned, breaking up any lumps with a fork or wooden spoon. Add the stock, raisins and chickpeas, stir well and simmer for 5 minutes. Stir in the tomato, coriander and mint; cover and keep warm.

2 To make Yoghurt Dressing: Place the yoghurt, coriander and lemon juice in a bowl and stir lightly. Keep chilled until serving.
3 Mix the turmeric and the remaining oil in a small dish and lightly brush over the eggplant halves. Heat a frying pan over medium heat. Add the eggplants in 1 layer and fry quickly, turning regularly and carefully with tongs until they are golden and the flesh is soft. Serve the mince topped with the eggplant halves and the Yoghurt Dressing.

Stir in the beef stock, raisins and drained chickpeas and simmer for 5 minutes.

Lightly brush the oil mixture over the eggplant halves with a pastry brush.

Fry the eggplants, turning regularly with tongs, until golden and soft.

LAMB AND FILO PIE

Preparation time: 40 minutes + cooling
Total cooking time: 1 hour
Serves 4–6

1 large onion, chopped
500 g (1 lb) lean lamb mince
1/2 teaspoon ground cinnamon
1/2 teaspoon ground allspice
1/4 cup (15 g/1/2 oz) finely
　chopped fresh parsley
1/3 cup (50 g/12/3 oz) pine nuts,
　toasted
2 tablespoons chopped
　fresh mint

3–4 teaspoons lemon juice
30 g (1 oz) butter, melted
12 sheets filo pastry

1 Heat a little oil in a heavy-based frying pan. Add the onion and cook for 3 minutes, or until soft and golden.
2 Add the lamb mince, breaking up any lumps with a fork or wooden spoon, and cook until brown. Stir in the cinnamon, allspice, parsley, pine nuts, mint and lemon juice. Season, to taste, with salt and pepper. Remove from the heat and allow to cool.
3 Preheat the oven to moderate 180°C (350°F/Gas 4). Combine the melted butter with a little olive oil and brush

a 30 x 18 cm (12 x 7 inch) baking dish. Layer 4 sheets of filo pastry together, brushing lightly between each layer with the butter and oil mixture. Place lengthways in the baking dish. Spread half the mince mixture over the pastry. Then top with another 4 sheets of buttered filo. Spread the remaining mince mixture over the pastry and top with the last 4 buttered sheets, tucking the pastry into the sides of the dish. Brush the top with the remaining butter and oil mixture. Score the top of the pastry diagonally into large squares, using a sharp knife. Bake for 45–50 minutes, or until golden.

Season the mince mixture with salt and pepper, to taste.

Arrange the filo pastry lengthways in the baking dish.

Cover half of the mince with filo and spread the remaining mince over the top.

TURKISH PIDE

Preparation time: 40 minutes
  + 1 hour 30 minutes resting
Total cooking time: 20 minutes
Serves 4

Pizza Dough
3 teaspoons caster sugar
7 g (1/4 oz) sachet dry yeast
3 1/2 cups (435 g/13 3/4 oz) plain
  flour
1/2 teaspoon salt
1/3 cup (80 ml/2 3/4 fl oz) olive oil

Topping
1 tablespoon oil
500 g (1 lb) lamb mince
2 teaspoons ground cumin
1 teaspoon ground cinnamon
2 tablespoons sultanas
1 tablespoon pine nuts
1/3 cup (90 g/3 oz) tomato paste
2 cups (130 g/4 1/4 oz) shredded
  English spinach
2 tablespoons fresh coriander
  leaves
200 g (6 1/2 oz) feta cheese,
  crumbled
1 egg, lightly beaten

1 To make Pizza Dough:
Combine the sugar and 1/3 cup
(80 ml/2 3/4 fl oz) warm water in a
small bowl. Stir in the yeast and set
aside in a warm, draught-free place
for 5 minutes, or until the mixture
begins to foam.
2 Place the flour and salt in a large
bowl, stir in the yeast mixture, olive
oil and 3/4 cup (185 ml/6 fl oz) warm
water and mix with a wooden spoon
until the mixture comes together.
Transfer the mixture to a lightly oiled
surface and knead for 12 minutes to
develop the gluten in the flour. Lightly
press the dough with your fingers. If
it springs back, it is ready.
3 Lightly oil a bowl and place the
dough inside. Cover the bowl tightly
with plastic wrap and put in a warm,
draught-free place for approximately
1–1 1/2 hours, or until the dough has
doubled in size.
4 Punch down the dough and remove
from the bowl. Divide into 4 portions
and shape into ovals. Roll out each
portion of dough on a lightly floured
surface to form an oval about 35 cm
(14 inches) long. Place the ovals on a
non-stick baking tray. Preheat the
oven to hot 220°C (425°F/Gas 7).
5 To make Topping: Heat the oil
in a non-stick frying pan, add the
lamb mince and cook over medium
heat for 8 minutes, breaking up any
lumps with a fork or wooden spoon.
Add the ground cumin and cinnamon,
sultanas and pine nuts and cook for 3
minutes. Remove from the heat and
allow to cool slightly.
6 Spread each dough oval with
tomato paste, leaving a 2 cm (3/4 inch)
border. Top with the English spinach,
mince mixture, coriander leaves and
feta cheese. Brush the edges of the
dough with the beaten egg and pinch
the ends together to form points that
hold the sides of the dough up.
Lightly brush the outside of the dough
with the remaining egg. Bake for
15 minutes, or until the dough is crisp
and golden.

COOK'S FILE

Note: If the mixture feels too moist,
work it on a lightly floured surface.
Variation: Pide can be made with
lots of different fillings. One variation
is to break an egg on top of each pide
just before baking.

*Set the yeast aside until the mixture
begins to foam.*

*Using a wooden spoon, stir the yeast,
olive oil and extra water into the flour.*

*Check that the dough is ready by pressing
it lightly. It should spring back.*

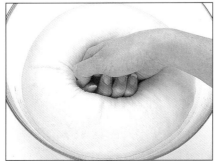

When the dough has risen, punch it down before dividing into four.

Stir the cumin, cinnamon, sultanas and pine nuts into the mince.

Use a flat-bladed knife to spread tomato paste over each oval.

SOMETHING DIFFERENT

PORK AND LEMON GRASS WON TONS

Preparation time: 40 minutes
  + 1 hour refrigeration
Total cooking time: 20 minutes
Makes 56

400 g (12²/₃ oz) pork mince
1 teaspoon finely chopped
  fresh ginger
1 stem lemon grass, white part
  only, finely sliced
230 g (7¹/₃ oz) can water
  chestnuts, drained and
  finely chopped
2 tablespoons finely chopped
  fresh garlic chives
¹/₂ teaspoon chilli paste
2 tablespoons plum sauce
1 teaspoon chilli oil
1 teaspoon sesame oil
1 tablespoon cornflour
56 x 8 cm (3 inch) won ton
  wrappers
oil, for deep-frying

Dipping Sauce
¹/₂ cup (125 ml/4 fl oz) light soy
  sauce
¹/₄ cup (60 ml/2 fl oz) balsamic
  vinegar
1 teaspoon finely grated fresh
  ginger
1 teaspoon chilli oil

1 In a bowl, combine the pork mince, ginger, lemon grass, water chestnuts, garlic chives, chilli paste, plum sauce, chilli and sesame oils and the cornflour. Mix well using your hands. Cover and refrigerate for 1 hour.

2 To make Dipping Sauce: Combine the soy sauce, balsamic vinegar, ginger and chilli oil in a jug and stir well.

3 Work with 1 won ton wrapper at a time, keeping the rest covered. Place about 2 teaspoons of the filling onto the centre of each wrapper and lightly brush the edges of the wrapper with water. Gather up the ends, bring the edges together in the centre and press firmly to seal. Repeat with the remaining wrappers and filling.

4 Deep-fry the won tons, in batches, in moderately hot oil for 3–4 minutes, or until lightly browned. Remove with a slotted spoon and drain well on paper towels. Serve hot with the Dipping Sauce.

Mix all the ingredients for the filling in a large bowl and then cover and refrigerate.

Place a ball of the mixture on a wrapper and brush the pastry edges with water.

BRUSCHETTA WITH ITALIAN BEEF

Preparation time: 40 minutes
Total cooking time: 20 minutes
Serves 4

1 small red onion, finely
    chopped
400 g (12²/₃ oz) lean beef mince
2 cloves garlic, crushed
¹/₃ cup (80 ml/2³/₄ fl oz) red
    wine
¹/₂ cup (125 ml/4 fl oz) chicken
    stock

2 teaspoons soft brown sugar
¹/₄ cup (40 g/1¹/₃ oz) pitted
    Kalamata olives, chopped
1 tablespoon fresh oregano leaves
2 large tomatoes
150 g (4³/₄ oz) rocket, shredded
1 teaspoon balsamic vinegar
1 teaspoon extra virgin olive oil
1 loaf Italian bread, sliced
    diagonally into 8 thick pieces
1 clove garlic, halved

1 Heat a little olive oil in a large
frying pan and cook the onion over
low heat until softened. Increase the
heat to high, add the mince and brown

well, breaking up any lumps with a
fork or wooden spoon. Add the
crushed garlic, red wine, stock, sugar
and olives to the pan. Simmer for
about 10 minutes, or until the liquid is
reduced and the meat is tender. Stir in
the oregano leaves and keep warm.
2 Chop the tomatoes into small pieces
and toss with the shredded rocket,
vinegar, olive oil and some salt and
black pepper, to taste.
3 Toast the slices of bread on both
sides and quickly rub with the clove
of garlic. Spoon the beef over 4 slices
of the bruschetta. On the other
4 slices, serve the tomato and rocket.

*Using a long knife, slice the bread
diagonally into 8 thick pieces.*

*Stir in the garlic, red wine, stock, sugar
and chopped olives.*

*Combine the tomato and rocket and then
toss in vinegar, oil and salt and pepper.*

MEATBALLS STIFADO

Preparation time: 40 minutes
Total cooking time: 1 hour 20 minutes
Serves 4

500 g (1 lb) lean beef mince
1 medium onion, grated
1 cup (80 g/2²/3 oz) fresh white
   breadcrumbs
2 teaspoons dried oregano
1 egg, beaten
3 tablespoons olive oil
2 cloves garlic, crushed
¹/2 teaspoon cumin seeds
¹/2 teaspoon ground cinnamon
1 teaspoon plain flour

2 cups (500 ml/16 fl oz) beef
   stock
1¹/2 tablespoons tomato paste
3 teaspoons soft brown sugar
2–3 bay leaves
12 Kalamata olives
100 g (3¹/3 oz) feta cheese,
   cut into small cubes
2 tablespoons finely chopped
   fresh flat-leaf parsley

1 Combine the beef mince, onion breadcrumbs and oregano in a bowl. Add the egg and mix well with your hands. Season with salt and pepper. Roll heaped tablespoons into balls.
2 Heat 1 tablespoon of oil in a pan and brown the meatballs over high heat, in batches if necessary. Transfer to a casserole dish. Preheat the oven to moderate 180°C (350°F/Gas 4).
3 Return the frying pan to low heat. Add the remaining oil and stir in the garlic, cumin seeds and cinnamon. Cook for 1 minute, stirring constantly, then add the flour and cook for another 30 seconds. Remove from the heat and gradually add the beef stock, stirring constantly. Return to the heat and bring to the boil before stirring in the tomato paste, brown sugar, bay leaves and olives. Pour the mixture over the meatballs. Cover and bake for 1 hour. Stir the feta through, sprinkle parsley over the top and serve with pasta or rice.

Roll heaped tablespoonsful of the meat mixture into balls.

Remove the pan from the heat and gradually stir in the beef stock.

Stir in the tomato paste, sugar, bay leaves and olives.

SWEET POTATO AND BEEF TURNOVERS

Preparation time: 45 minutes
Total cooking time: 45 minutes
Serves 4

1 tablespoon oil
1 tablespoon Madras curry paste
1 clove garlic, crushed
1 onion, finely chopped
1 green capsicum, seeded and
    finely chopped
500 g (1 lb) lean beef mince
1 tablespoon plain flour
425 g (13¹/₂ oz) can crushed
    tomatoes

1 teaspoon beef stock powder
400 g (12²/₃ oz) sweet potato,
    diced
4 sheets ready-rolled puff pastry
1 egg, lightly beaten
3 tablespoons polenta

1 Heat the oil in a large frying pan, add the curry paste, garlic, onion and capsicum and stir for 2–3 minutes. Transfer to a bowl. Add the beef mince to the pan and cook over a high heat for 5–6 minutes, or until brown, breaking up any lumps with a fork or wooden spoon. Stir in the flour and return the capsicum mixture to the pan. Add the tomatoes, stock powder and sweet potato. Mix well, reduce the heat and simmer for 12–15 minutes, stirring occasionally. Remove from the heat and allow to cool. Preheat the oven to moderately hot 200°C (400°F/Gas 6).

2 Cut each sheet of pastry into a 24 cm (9¹/₂ inch) diameter circle. Spoon the cooled filling over half of each circle. Brush the edge of each circle with beaten egg and fold the pastry over the filling to form a semi-circle. Pinch the edges together.

3 Transfer to 2 oven trays that have been oiled and dusted with the polenta. Brush each turnover with beaten egg and sprinkle with the polenta. Bake for 20–25 minutes, or until crisp and golden.

Add tomatoes, stock powder and sweet potato to the meat and capsicum mixture.

Cut around an upside-down bowl to make 24 cm circles from the sheets of pastry.

Brush the edge of each pastry with beaten egg and fold it over the filling.

OLIVE BEEF BALLS WITH TOMATO SAUCE

Preparation time: 30 minutes
+ 30 minutes refrigeration
Total cooking time: 30 minutes
Makes 30

600 g (1¼ lb) lean beef mince
1 cup (80 g/2⅔ oz) fresh
  breadcrumbs
1 egg, lightly beaten
30 stuffed green olives
fresh oregano sprigs, to garnish

Tomato Sauce
2 cloves garlic, crushed
425 g (13½ oz) can peeled
  tomatoes
45 g (1½ oz) can anchovy fillets
  in olive oil
2 tablespoons red wine

1 Mix together the beef mince, breadcrumbs, egg and some salt and pepper. Roll a level tablespoon of the mixture into a ball and then flatten to a disc about 1 cm (½ inch) thick. Place an olive on the meat and enclose it completely, rerolling to form a firm ball. Repeat with remaining mixture to make 30 balls. Refrigerate for at least 30 minutes.
2 Preheat the oven to moderate 180°C (350°F/Gas 4). Cover a large oven tray with foil, place the meatballs on it and bake for 20 minutes, turning once during cooking.
3 To make Tomato Sauce: Process all the ingredients in a food processor or blender until smooth. Pour into a small pan, bring to the boil and simmer over low heat for 10 minutes, stirring occasionally. Serve warm over the beef balls and garnish with a few oregano sprigs.

COOK'S FILE

Note: To make fresh breadcrumbs, remove the crusts from day-old bread, break the bread into small pieces and then either rub between your hands or process in a food processor.

Press an olive onto each disc of meat and then roll the meat into a ball around it.

Put the meatballs on a foil-lined tray and bake, turning once during cooking.

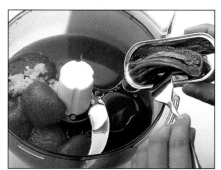

Place all the Tomato Sauce ingredients in a food processor and blend until smooth.

CHICKEN DUMPLINGS IN GREEN CURRY

Preparation time: 25 minutes
 + 2–3 hours refrigeration
Total cooking time: 35 minutes
Serves 3–4

500 g (1 lb) chicken mince
3 spring onions, finely chopped
2 tablespoons small fresh
   coriander leaves
1 stem lemon grass, white part
   only, finely sliced
3 tablespoons fish sauce
1 teaspoon chicken stock
   powder

1½ cups (280 g/9 oz) cooked
   jasmine rice
1 egg, plus 1 egg white
2 teaspoons oil
2 tablespoons green curry paste
2 x 400 ml (12 ⅔ fl oz) cans
   coconut milk
4 fresh kaffir lime leaves
½ cup (25 g/¾ oz) fresh basil
   leaves
1 tablespoon lemon juice

1 Mix together the chicken mince, spring onion, coriander leaves, lemon grass, 2 tablespoons of the fish sauce, stock powder and some pepper. Add the rice and mix well with your hands.
2 In a separate bowl, beat the egg and egg white with electric beaters until thick and creamy and then fold into the chicken mixture. With lightly floured hands, roll tablespoons of the mixture into balls. Place on a tray, cover and refrigerate for 2–3 hours, or until firm.
3 Heat the oil in a large frying pan, add the green curry paste and stir over medium heat for 1 minute. Gradually stir in the coconut milk, then reduce the heat to simmer. Add the lime leaves and chicken dumplings to the sauce; cover and simmer for 25–30 minutes, stirring occasionally. Stir in the basil leaves, remaining fish sauce and lemon juice. Serve with steamed rice.

Beat the egg and egg white until thick and creamy.

Flour your hands and roll tablespoons of the mixture into balls.

When the sauce is simmering, add the lime leaves and chicken balls.

MUSHROOM, MINCE AND FETA STRUDEL

Preparation time: 50 minutes
Total cooking time: 35–40 minutes
Serves 6

1 tablespoon olive oil
6 slices pancetta or very thinly
   sliced smoked bacon, chopped
150 g (4³/4 oz) baby button
   mushrooms, stalks trimmed
4 spring onions, finely chopped
500 g (1 lb) chicken mince
¹/2 cup (125 ml/4 fl oz) chicken
   stock
1 tablespoon chopped fresh
   sage leaves
150 g (4³/4 oz) feta cheese,
   cut into small cubes
8 sheets filo pastry
80 g (2²/3 oz) butter, melted
³/4 cup (60 g/2 oz) very finely
   ground fresh breadcrumbs

1 Heat the oil in a frying pan, add the pancetta, mushrooms and spring onion and cook for 2 minutes, stirring regularly. Add the chicken mince and cook over high heat until it changes colour, breaking up any lumps with a fork or wooden spoon.
2 Add the stock, reduce the heat and simmer for 3 minutes, or until the liquid has been absorbed. Stir in the sage, transfer to a bowl and cool for 10 minutes before adding the feta.
3 Preheat the oven to moderately hot 200°C (400°F/Gas 6). Lightly brush an oven tray with some melted butter or oil. Work with 1 sheet of filo at a time, covering the remainder with a damp tea towel to prevent them drying out. Brush the sheet lightly with the melted butter and sprinkle with

breadcrumbs. Repeat with the remaining pastry sheets, butter and breadcrumbs, reserving 2 tablespoons of the breadcrumbs. Spoon the mince filling along the centre of the pastry and fold in the edges. Firmly, but gently, roll up the pastry, place seam-side-down on the tray and brush with butter. Cut slashes along the top of the

parcel and sprinkle with the remaining breadcrumbs. Bake for 20–25 minutes, or until golden. Leave for 5 minutes before cutting.

COOK'S FILE

Note: Cool the filling completely before rolling up in the pastry or the filo will become soggy.

Add the cubed feta to the cooled meat mixture and mix through gently.

Sprinkle the sheets of buttered filo pastry with breadcrumbs.

Spoon the cooled mince filling along the centre of the filo pastry.

75

CRACKED WHEAT AND LAMB BURGER

Preparation time: 25 minutes
+ 30 minutes standing
Total cooking time: 5–10 minutes
Serves 4

1/4 cup (45 g/1 1/2 oz) burghul
(cracked wheat)
400 g (12 2/3 oz) lean lamb mince
1 tablespoon lime juice
2 teaspoons grated lime rind
1/3 cup (20 g/2/3 oz) finely
chopped fresh parsley
3 cloves garlic, crushed
4 tablespoons chopped fresh
mint
2–3 tablespoons oil
1 large red onion, finely
chopped
1 large tomato, finely chopped
1 teaspoon soft brown sugar
4 bread rolls
salad leaves and plain yoghurt,
for serving

1 Soak the cracked wheat in 1/4 cup (60 ml/2 fl oz) water for 30 minutes. Drain and squeeze out the excess water. Using your hands, mix together the burghul with the lamb mince, lime juice and rind, parsley, 2 cloves of garlic, 2 tablespoons of mint and plenty of salt and freshly ground black pepper. Divide the mixture into 4 and shape into patties.

2 Heat the oil in a large frying pan. Add the lamb patties and cook for 3–4 minutes each side, or until brown and cooked through.

3 Mix the onion, tomato, remaining garlic and mint, brown sugar and some salt and black pepper in a bowl. Fill the rolls with the salad leaves, a patty, some of the onion and tomato mixture and a spoonful of yoghurt.

Soak the cracked wheat in water for about 30 minutes, to soften.

Divide the mixture into 4 and shape into patties.

Mix together the onion, tomato, garlic, mint, sugar and some salt and pepper.

BARBECUED TUNA BURGER

Preparation time: 15 minutes
+ 2 hours refrigeration
Total cooking time: 10 minutes
Serves 4

700 g (1 lb 6 2/3 oz) fresh tuna
3 spring onions, finely chopped
1 tablespoon mirin
1 teaspoon soy sauce
1 tablespoon lime juice

1 Finely chop the tuna until it resembles mince. Mix in a bowl with the spring onion, mirin, soy sauce and lime juice.

2 Divide the mixture into 4 and shape into round patties. Cover with some plastic wrap and refrigerate for 2 hours.

3 Cook the patties on a preheated chargrill pan or barbecue grill or flatplate for 8–10 minutes, or until cooked through, turning once. Serve hot or cold with wedges of lime, your favourite relish and salad leaves.

COOK'S FILE

Note: This recipe can also be used to make tiny tuna meatballs for serving with drinks. With wet hands, shape heaped tablespoons of the mince mixture into balls and refrigerate for 2 hours. Preheat the oven to moderate 180°C (350°F/Gas 4). Then add a little oil to a large non-stick frying pan and cook in batches for 3 minutes, or until just brown. Place the meatballs on a non-stick baking tray and complete the cooking by baking in the oven for 5 minutes.

Use a large, sharp knife to chop the tuna until it resembles mince.

Place the tuna patties on a plate, cover with plastic wrap and refrigerate.

Cook the patties for 8–10 minutes, or until cooked through. Turn them once.

*Cracked Wheat and Lamb Burger (top)
with Barbecued Tuna Burger*

Party Pieces

BEEF KEBABS

Combine 375 g (12 oz) lean beef mince, 150 g (4¾ oz) pork and veal mince, 1 small finely chopped onion, 1 egg yolk, 1–2 cloves crushed garlic, 1 tablespoon plum sauce, 1 tablespoon tomato sauce, 2 teaspoons mustard, 2 tablespoons finely chopped fresh chives and salt and freshly ground black pepper. Mix with your hands until the mixture is well combined and has come together. Roll 2 teaspoons of the mixture into small balls with wet hands. Mould 2 balls onto small skewers, then cook under a preheated grill for 5–10 minutes, turning occasionally, until browned and cooked through. Serve the meatballs with a dipping sauce. Makes 28–30.

Left to right: Beef Kebabs; Mini Koftas;
Herbed Beef en Croute; Pastry Fingers

MINI KOFTAS

In a large bowl, soak ¼ cup (45 g/1½ oz) burghul in 250 ml (8 fl oz) water for about 30 minutes. After soaking, drain the burghul and squeeze out the excess liquid. Combine the burghul in a medium bowl with 750 g (1½ lb) lean minced lamb or beef, 1 small finely chopped onion, 1–2 cloves crushed garlic, 2 teaspoons ground cumin, ½ teaspoon ground cinnamon, 3 tablespoons finely chopped toasted pine nuts, 1 tablespoon finely chopped fresh mint and 1 egg. Combine the ingredients well with your hands until the mixture is smooth. Then wet your hands and roll tablespoons of the mixture into small sausage shapes. Mould these sausages lengthways onto short skewers. Cook the Koftas under a preheated grill, turning regularly, for 5–10 minutes, or until they are browned all over and cooked through. Serve hot with a yoghurt dipping sauce or a bowl of hummus. Makes 40.

HERBED BEEF EN CROUTE

Heat a large frying pan with a little oil and butter. Add 2 onions, cut into thin rings. Cook over medium heat until dark golden brown, but not burnt. Set aside and keep warm. Meanwhile, combine 440 g (14 oz) lean beef mince in a bowl with 3 tablespoons chopped fresh parsley, salt, lots of freshly ground black pepper or 1 tablespoon crushed green peppercorns, and 1 finely chopped spring onion. Mix well with your hands. Shape tablespoons of the mixture into round, flat patties. Cook the patties either in a frying pan or under a preheated grill for 2–3 minutes each side, or until browned and cooked through. Cut 1 small, thin French bread stick into 20 x 1 cm (1/2 inch) diagonal slices. Toast under a preheated grill until golden. Then combine 1/2 cup (125 g/4 oz) sour cream with 2–3 teaspoons hot English mustard or horseradish cream. Spread a little of this mixture onto each slice of the French bread. Top with a mini beef patty and some of the cooked onion. Sprinkle with a little extra chopped parsley to garnish. Makes 20.

Note: This recipe is also delicious made with chicken mince instead of beef.

PASTRY FINGERS

Heat a little olive oil in a large frying pan. Add 300 g (9²/3 oz) lamb mince and cook over medium heat until brown, breaking up any lumps with a fork or wooden spoon. Stir in 1–2 cloves crushed garlic, 3 teaspoons each of ground cumin and coriander, 3 finely chopped spring onions and 2 tablespoons finely chopped raisins. Cook for another 3 minutes and remove from the heat. Stir in 4 tablespoons grated Cheddar cheese, 2–3 teaspoons chopped fresh mint and season with salt and freshly ground black pepper. Allow the mixture to cool slightly. Brush a sheet of filo pastry lightly with a little combined melted butter and oil. Cover with another sheet. Cut the pastry sheet into 9 squares. Brush each square with more butter and oil. Spoon 1 tablespoon of the mince mixture along 1 edge of each pastry square. Fold in the edges and roll up into a fat cigar shape. Place pastries on a greased baking tray, seam-side-down. Repeat with more filo sheets until all the mixture has been used up. Bake in a preheated moderate 180°C (350°F/Gas 4) oven for 10 minutes, or until golden brown. Makes 16–18.

Party Pieces

PRAWN TOASTS

Add 345 g (11 oz) raw prawn meat, 1–2 cloves peeled garlic, 60 g (2 oz) drained water chestnuts, 1 tablespoon chopped fresh coriander, 1–2 teaspoons grated fresh ginger, 1 stem finely chopped lemon grass (white part only), 2 egg whites and 1 teaspoon soy sauce to a food processor or blender and process until smooth. Cut rounds of white sliced bread with a 5 cm (2 inch) diameter cutter. Brush 1 side of each round with a little beaten egg yolk, then spread evenly with some of the prawn mixture and sprinkle with sesame seeds. Deep-fry the toasts in moderately hot oil with the prawn mixture facing downwards, for 5–7 minutes, or until they are golden brown and crisp. You will need to deep-fry the toasts in small batches. Make sure that both sides of the toasts are cooked, then remove them from the pan and drain well on paper towels. Serve immediately with a dipping sauce. Makes 30–35.

CHIPOLATAS WITH SPICY SAUCE

In a large, heavy-based pan, combine 1 kg (2 lb) ripe, chopped tomatoes, 1 large finely chopped onion, 1/2 cup (125 ml/4 fl oz) cider vinegar, 1 cup (185 g/6 oz) lightly packed soft brown sugar, 1/4 cup (60 ml/2 fl oz) Worcestershire sauce, 1 teaspoon ground allspice, 3/4 teaspoon ground ginger, 1/4 teaspoon ground cloves, salt and freshly ground black pepper. Bring the mixture to the boil, reduce the heat and simmer for about 40 minutes, stirring occasionally. Cool slightly, then process in batches until smooth. Heat a frying pan with a little oil and butter. Add 1–2 cloves crushed garlic and cook for 1 minute. Add 1 kg (2 lb) chipolata sausages and cook over medium heat for 3–4 minutes, or until browned and cooked through. Serve immediately with the warm or cold sauce. This recipe makes 750 ml (24 fl oz) of Spicy Sauce and any leftover Sauce can be refrigerated.

COCKTAIL MEATBALLS WITH TZATZIKI

In a large bowl, add 750 g (1½ lb) beef or lamb mince, 1 large grated onion, 1½ cups (120 g/4 oz) fresh white breadcrumbs, 2 cloves crushed garlic, 2 teaspoons ground cumin, 1 teaspoon cumin seeds, 1 teaspoon dried oregano leaves, 2 tablespoons finely chopped fresh parsley, 1 lightly beaten egg and salt, to taste. Combine the mixture well with your hands. Then wet your hands and shape the mixture into small meatballs, using about 2 teaspoons of the mixture for each one. In a large frying pan, heat 2 tablespoons olive oil. Add the meatballs in small batches and fry until golden and cooked through, turning them while they cook to evenly brown them. Transfer to a warmed serving dish and sprinkle with some lemon juice and salt. Meanwhile, make the Tzatziki by mixing together in a large bowl 1 cup (250 g/8 oz) thick plain yoghurt, ¼ telegraph cucumber, grated and squeezed to remove excess juices, 1 clove crushed garlic, 1 teaspoon olive oil and 1 tablespoon finely chopped fresh mint or dill. Pour the Tzatziki into a serving bowl and serve with the meatballs. Makes 80 meatballs.

WON TON CRISPS

In a small bowl, mix together 155 g (5 oz) pork and veal mince, 1 tablespoon finely chopped fresh coriander, 1 clove crushed garlic, 2–3 teaspoons soy sauce, 1 tablespoon plum sauce, salt and some freshly ground black pepper. Place 1 teaspoon of the mixture towards the corner of a square won ton wrapper. Brush around the corner edge with a little water and then fold the corner over. Press the wrapper firmly to seal, leaving a large edge. Continue this process with the remaining mixture and won ton wrappers until the mixture is finished. Then deep-fry the won tons in moderately hot oil until they are crisp and golden brown. You may need to do this in small batches, depending on the size of your pan. Remove the won tons with tongs and drain them well on paper towels. Serve with a dipping sauce. Makes 32.

Left to right: Prawn Toasts; Chipolatas with Spicy Sauce; Cocktail Meatballs with Tzatziki; Won Ton Crisps

BEEF AND KIDNEY BEAN BURRITO BAKE

Preparation time: 25 minutes
Total cooking time: 1 hour
Serves 4

1 tablespoon oil
1 green chilli, seeded and finely
    chopped
1 red onion, chopped
500 g (1 lb) lean beef mince
420 g (13¼ oz) can kidney
    beans, drained and rinsed
425 g (13½ oz) can chopped
    tomatoes
450 g (14⅓ oz) can refried
    beans
½ teaspoon garam masala
1 teaspoon cumin seeds
4 x 30 cm (12 inch) flour
    tortillas
⅓ cup (90 g/3 oz) sour cream
135 g (4½ oz) Cheddar
    cheese, grated

1 Heat the oil in a large pan, add the green chilli and onion and stir for 1 minute. Increase the heat and add the beef mince. Cook for 4–5 minutes, or until the meat is just brown, breaking up any lumps with a fork or wooden spoon.
2 Stir in the kidney beans, tomatoes, refried beans, garam masala and cumin seeds. Reduce the heat and simmer gently for 25–30 minutes, stirring occasionally.
3 Preheat the oven to moderate 180°C (350°F/Gas 4). Divide the filling into 4 equal portions and spoon one portion down the centre of each tortilla. Then roll the tortilla up to enclose the filling.
4 Lightly brush a large ovenproof dish with melted butter or oil. Place the filled tortillas seam-side-down in the dish, spread evenly with the sour cream and sprinkle with Cheddar cheese. Bake for 20–25 minutes, or until the cheese has melted and started to brown and the burritos are slightly crispy. Serve immediately.

COOK'S FILE

Note: Flour tortillas are available in many supermarkets. If you can't find them, you could replace the tortillas with pitta bread.

Add the mince to the chilli and onion and cook until lightly browned.

Stir in kidney beans, tomatoes, refried beans, garam masala and cumin seeds.

Spoon a line of filling down the centre of each of the tortillas.

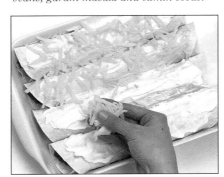

Spread sour cream on top of the filled tortillas and sprinkle with grated cheese.

SPICY PORK WON TONS

Preparation time: 25 minutes
Total cooking time: 10 minutes
Serves 4–6

1 teaspoon sesame oil
1 teaspoon peanut oil
2 cloves garlic, crushed
2 spring onions, finely chopped
2 small red chillies, finely
    chopped
2 teaspoons grated fresh ginger
300 g (9²/₃ oz) pork mince
1 tablespoon hoisin sauce
2 tablespoons unsalted peanuts,
    chopped

1 tablespoon chopped fresh
    coriander
250 g (8 oz) won ton wrappers
oil, for deep-frying

Sauce
1/2 cup (125 ml/4 fl oz) salt-
    reduced soy sauce
1 tablespoon soft brown sugar
1 teaspoon chilli oil

1 Heat both oils in a non-stick frying pan. Add the garlic, spring onion, chilli and ginger and cook over medium heat for 2 minutes. Increase the heat to high, add the pork mince and cook, breaking up any lumps with a fork or wooden spoon, for 5 minutes, or until the mince is brown. Remove the pan from the heat and stir in hoisin, peanuts and coriander. Place 2 teaspoons of the mixture into the centre of 1 wrapper, brush the border of the won ton lightly with water, place another wrapper on top. Repeat the procedure with the remaining wrappers and pork mince.

2 Deep-fry the won tons in batches for 3 minutes, or until crisp and golden. Drain on paper towels.

3 To make Sauce: Place the soy sauce, brown sugar and chilli oil into a small pan and simmer over medium heat for 5 minutes, or until the sauce thickens slightly. Pour into a bowl and serve with the won tons.

Take the pan off the heat and stir hoisin, peanuts and coriander into the mince.

Brush the edge of a won ton with water and place another wrapper on top.

Deep-fry the won tons until crisp. Place on paper towels to drain off excess oil.

PORK, FENNEL AND CHILLI SAUSAGES

Preparation time: 25 minutes
Total cooking time: 30 minutes
Serves 4–6

1 teaspoon fennel seeds
1 kg (2 lb) pork mince
2 cloves garlic, crushed
1 cup (140 g/4²/3 oz) grated
    fresh fennel bulb
1 teaspoon ground cumin
1¹/2 teaspoons chilli powder
1 teaspoon sweet paprika

1 tablespoon fresh lemon
    thyme leaves
1 tablespoon oil

Apple Yoghurt Sauce
200 g (6¹/2 oz) thick plain
    yoghurt
1 apple, peeled and grated
1 tablespoon chopped fresh dill

1 Preheat the oven to moderate 180°C (350°F/Gas 4). Dry-roast the fennel seeds in a small frying pan over medium heat until they begin to pop.
2 In a large bowl, combine the roasted fennel seeds, pork mince,

garlic, fennel, cumin, chilli, sweet paprika, lemon thyme leaves and some salt and pepper, to taste. Mix together well using your hands. Divide the mixture into 12 equal portions and shape each portion into a sausage 12 cm (5 inches) long.
3 Heat the oil in a large non-stick frying pan and cook the sausages in batches until brown. Complete the cooking by baking the sausages on a non-stick baking tray for 10 minutes, turning occasionally.
4 To make Apple Yoghurt Sauce: Combine the yoghurt, apple and dill in a bowl. Serve with the sausages.

Place all the ingredients, apart from the oil, in a large bowl and mix thoroughly.

Mould each portion of the mixture into a 12 cm long sausage.

Cook the sausages in the oil until brown, then bake in the oven for 10 minutes.

FRESH SALMON TARTARE

Preparation time: 20 minutes
Total cooking time: Nil
Serves 4

400 g (12²/3 oz) fresh salmon
    fillet
2 spring onions, finely chopped
1 tablespoon tiny capers
    or finely chopped
    regular capers

1 tablespoon finely chopped
    gherkin
fresh chopped dill, to garnish
1 lemon, cut into wedges

1 Remove the skin and any connective tissue or bones from the salmon. This should leave you with approximately 70 g (2¹/3 oz) of fish per person. Using a large, sharp knife, finely chop the salmon until it has the texture of mince.
2 Place the salmon mince in a bowl with the spring onion, capers, gherkin

and some salt and freshly ground black pepper, to taste. Refrigerate, covered, until just before serving.
3 When ready to serve, roughly pile onto individual plates and sprinkle with the dill. Grind some more black pepper over the fish and serve with a wedge of lemon. This should be accompanied by some buttered rye bread or lightly toasted pitta bread.

C O O K ' S   F I L E

Note: You can also make this dish with fresh tuna.

Use a sharp knife to remove the skin and any connective tissue or bones.

Chop the salmon up finely until it resembles mince.

Mix spring onion, capers, gherkin and salt and pepper into the salmon mince.

*Pork, Fennel and Chilli Sausages (top)
with Fresh Salmon Tartare*

ORANGE CHILLI CHICKEN IN LETTUCE CUPS

Preparation time: 35–40 minutes
Total cooking time: 10–15 minutes
Serves 4

500 g (1 lb) chicken mince
1 tablespoon soy sauce
1 tablespoon rice wine vinegar
1 tablespoon sesame oil
peanut oil, for deep-frying
60 g (2 oz) dried rice vermicelli
   noodles, broken in sections
1 red capsicum, finely chopped
115 g (3³⁄4 oz) can water
   chestnuts, drained and
   coarsely chopped
2 spring onions, finely sliced
1 teaspoon grated fresh ginger
1 iceberg or romaine lettuce

Sauce
2 tablespoons soy sauce
1 tablespoon teriyaki sauce
1 tablespoon mild-hot chilli sauce
2 tablespoons hoisin sauce
1 teaspoon sesame oil
2 teaspoons finely grated
   orange rind
1 teaspoon cornflour

1 Mix together the chicken mince, soy sauce, vinegar and sesame oil, cover and refrigerate.

2 Half-fill a wok, deep-fryer or large, heavy-based pan with oil and heat to moderately hot. Add the rice noodles in small batches (they increase in size rapidly, causing the oil to rise) and fry for 1–2 seconds, or until puffed. Remove and drain on paper towels.

3 To make Sauce: Combine all the ingredients and stir until the cornflour has dissolved. Set aside.

4 Heat a little peanut oil in a wok or large pan. Add the chicken mixture and fry for 3–4 minutes, breaking up any lumps with a fork or wooden spoon. Add the capsicum, water chestnuts, spring onion and ginger to the pan and toss for 1–2 minutes. Add the Sauce to the pan and stir for about 1 minute, or until slightly thickened. Remove from the heat and mix in the noodles, reserving a few for garnish. Form the lettuce leaves into 6–8 cups and divide the chicken mixture among them. Sprinkle the reserved noodles on top.

Finely slice 2 spring onions, including the green tops.

Use a slotted spoon to remove the cooked noodles from the pan.

Use a wooden spoon or fork to break up any lumps of mince as it cooks.

RED CAPSICUM AND CHICKEN TERRINE

Preparation time: 30 minutes
+ 30 minutes cooling
Total cooking time: 2 hours 10 minutes
Serves 6–8

500 g (1 lb) silver beet leaves,
stems removed
4 large red capsicums
1 kg (2 lb) chicken thigh fillets
1 tablespoon fresh lemon thyme
leaves
2 cloves garlic, crushed
2 spring onions, finely chopped
3 eggs, lightly beaten
1/2 cup (125 ml/4 fl oz) white
wine
1 tablespoon green peppercorns
1/4 cup (15 g/1/2 oz) chopped
fresh herbs
5 hard-boiled eggs, peeled

1 Preheat the oven to moderate 180°C (350°F/Gas 4). Steam the silver beet leaves for 3 minutes, or until tender, drain and squeeze out the excess moisture. Cut the capsicums into big, flat pieces, remove the seeds and membrane and brush the skin lightly with oil. Grill, skin-side-up, until the skin blisters and blackens. Seal in a plastic bag or cover with a tea towel until cool. Peel away the skin.
2 Line an 11 x 30 cm (4½ x 12 inch) loaf tin with foil, allowing it to overhang the sides of the tin. Line the base and sides with silver beet leaves, letting the leaves overlap the sides. Cover the silver beet leaves with two-thirds of the red capsicum on the base and sides of the tin.
3 Mince the chicken fillets in a food processor and transfer to a large bowl.

Mix in the lemon thyme, garlic, spring onion, beaten eggs, wine, peppercorns, herbs and salt and pepper.
4 Spoon half the mince into the lined tin. Position the hard-boiled eggs along the centre of the mince and spread the remaining mince evenly over the top. Cover with the rest of the capsicum, fold over the overlapping

silver beet leaves to encase the terrine and cover with the overlapping foil. Place the tin in a baking dish with enough hot water to come halfway up the sides of the tin. Bake for 2 hours. Remove from the water bath and drain off any excess juices. Weigh down with cans and set aside to cool slightly for 30 minutes.

Grill the capsicum pieces until the skin blackens and blisters.

Line the foil-lined tin with silver beet leaves, allowing them to overlap the sides.

Arrange the hard-boiled eggs along the centre of the layer of mince.

STUFFED VINE LEAVES

Preparation time: 1 hour
Total cooking time: 1 hour 20 minutes
Makes approximately 24

120 g (4 oz) packet of vine
    leaves in brine
2 tablespoons olive oil
150 g (4³/₄ oz) lean lamb mince
1 small onion, grated
2 cloves garlic, crushed
¼ cup (50 g/1²/₃ oz) white rice
1 tablespoon currants
½ teaspoon ground cinnamon
1 tablespoon pine nuts
½ cup (125 ml/4 fl oz) chicken
    stock or water
1 tablespoon chopped fresh
    parsley
1 tablespoon chopped fresh mint
1 tablespoon chopped fresh dill,
    optional
1 egg, lightly beaten
juice of 1 lemon
1 tablespoon sugar
3 cups (750 ml/24 fl oz) water

Egg and Lemon Sauce
2 eggs
juice of 1 lemon
1 cup (250 ml/8 fl oz) chicken
    stock

1 Soak the vine leaves in hot water for 10 minutes, rinse and drain.
2 Heat half the oil in a frying pan, add the lamb mince and brown well. Stir in the grated onion and crushed garlic and cook for 1 minute. Add the rice, currants, cinnamon and pine nuts to the pan and mix well. Pour in the stock or water and cook for 5 minutes. Stir the parsley, mint and dill, if using, through the mixture. Season with salt and black pepper, to taste. Allow to cool a little before stirring in the egg.
3 Place the vine leaves, vein-side-up, on a work surface and spoon about 2 teaspoons of the rice mixture onto the centre of each leaf. The amount of stuffing will depend on the size of the vine leaves. Fold the bottom of the leaf and the 2 sides into the centre. Then roll the whole leaf up towards the top point of the leaf.
4 Carefully place the stuffed vine leaves in a large pan, seam-side-down, and pour the lemon juice, remaining oil and sugar over the top. On top of this, position a dinner plate to hold the vine leaves in shape, and then pour in the water. The vine leaves should be just covered with liquid.
5 Bring the water to the boil, reduce heat to low and simmer for 1 hour. Transfer the cooked stuffed vine leaves to a serving dish.
6 **To make Egg and Lemon Sauce:** Whisk the eggs and lemon juice in a bowl. Place the stock in a pan and bring to the boil. Reduce the heat and keep warm. Gradually whisk ½ cup (125 ml/4 fl oz) of the hot stock into the egg mixture. Pour this mixture into the pan containing the remaining stock. Whisk over low heat for 2–3 minutes, or until the sauce thickens. Remove from the heat as soon as the sauce thickens as it will continue to cook in the pan. If the egg begins to cook in the sauce, quickly pour through a sieve, which cools the sauce and removes any cooked strands of egg. Serve with the Stuffed Vine Leaves.

COOK'S FILE

Note: You could also use 24 fresh young vine leaves. Blanch them in boiling water to soften.

Soak the vine leaves in hot water and then rinse well to remove excess salt.

Add the rice, currants, cinnamon and pine nuts to the mixture in the pan.

Lay out a vine leaf, vein-side-up, and put 2 teaspoons of the mixture in the centre.

Fold the bottom and 2 sides of the leaf into the centre; roll the leaf up to the tip.

Place stuffed vine leaves in a large pan and pour over lemon juice, oil and sugar.

For the Egg and Lemon Sauce, whisk 1/2 cup hot stock into the egg mixture.

CHICKEN RAVIOLI WITH FRESH TOMATO SAUCE

Preparation time: 40 minutes
Total cooking time: 40 minutes
Serves 4

Tomato Sauce
1 large onion, chopped
2 cloves garlic, crushed
1/3 cup (90 g/3 oz) tomato paste
1/4 cup (60 ml/2 fl oz) red wine
2/3 cup (170 ml/5 1/2 fl oz)
    chicken stock
2 medium tomatoes, chopped
1 tablespoon chopped fresh basil

Ravioli
200 g (6 1/2 oz) chicken mince
1 tablespoon chopped fresh basil
1/4 cup (25 g/3/4 oz) grated
    Parmesan
3 spring onions, finely chopped
50 g (1 2/3 oz) fresh ricotta
    cheese
250 g (8 oz) packet (48) round
    won ton or gow gee wrappers

1 To make Tomato Sauce: Heat about 1 tablespoon of oil in a pan and add the onion and garlic. Cook for 2–3 minutes, then stir in the tomato paste, wine, stock and tomato and simmer for 20 minutes. Stir in the

basil and season with salt and freshly ground black pepper.

2 To make Ravioli: Combine the chicken mince, basil, Parmesan, spring onion, ricotta and some salt and black pepper. Lay 24 of the wrappers on a flat surface and brush with a little water. Place slightly heaped teaspoons of the mixture onto the centre of each wrapper. Place another wrapper on top and press the edges firmly together.

3 Bring a large pan of water to the boil. Add the ravioli, a few at a time, and cook for 2–3 minutes, or until just tender. Drain well and serve with the Tomato Sauce.

For the Tomato Sauce, add the basil, salt and pepper to the tomato mixture.

For the Ravioli, combine the Parmesan, chicken, basil, spring onion and ricotta.

Place the mixture between two wrappers and press together to make the Ravioli.

VEGETABLE-TOPPED MINCE AND POLENTA PIE

Preparation time: 50 minutes + cooling
Total cooking time: 1 hour 20 minutes
Serves 6

2/3 cup (100 g/3¹/3 oz) coarsely-
    ground polenta
30 g (1 oz) butter
60 g (2 oz) Parmesan, grated
3 cloves garlic, finely chopped
2 small red onions
500 g (1 lb) lean lamb mince
1 small red capsicum, chopped
1 small zucchini, chopped
1 egg tomato, cut into quarters
2 tablespoons chopped fresh
    parsley
2 tablespoons olive oil
2 tablespoons shredded fresh
    basil leaves

1 Lightly grease a round 20 cm (8 inch) pie dish or a small square ovenproof dish.

2 Bring 2¹/4 cups (560 ml/18 fl oz) water to a rapid boil in a pan, sprinkle in the polenta and stir. Cook for 15 minutes over medium heat, stirring constantly, until the mixture forms a ball away from the sides of the pan and the spoon stands up by itself in the mixture. Stir in the butter and Parmesan and season well with salt and pepper. Pour into the base of the dish, smooth the top and set aside.

3 Heat about 2 tablespoons of oil in a frying pan, add the garlic and 1 finely chopped red onion and cook over medium heat for 5 minutes, or until golden. Add the mince and cook over high heat, stirring frequently, until brown. Drain on paper towels and spread over the polenta.

4 Preheat the oven to moderate 180°C (350°F/Gas 4). Arrange the remaining onion, cut into wedges, capsicum, zucchini and egg tomato over the mince and sprinkle with the parsley. Drizzle a little of the olive oil over the top and bake for 30 minutes. Drizzle the remaining oil over the top, sprinkle with basil and bake for another 15–20 minutes, or until the vegetables are just tender. Season

with salt and black pepper and cool for 20 minutes. Serve just warm.

COOK'S FILE

Hint: If you prefer, you can remove the skin from the capsicum. Cut the capsicum into quarters, remove the seeds and lightly brush the skin with oil. Grill, skin-side-up, until the skin blisters and blackens. Seal in a plastic bag until cool, then remove the skin.

Add the polenta to boiling water and cook over medium heat.

Drain the mince using paper towels and spread smoothly over the polenta.

Arrange the onion, capsicum, zucchini and egg tomato over the mince.

CHICKEN AND LIME HUMMUS TORTILLAS

Preparation time: 45 minutes
+ 30 minutes refrigeration
Total cooking time: 10–15 minutes
Serves 4

500 g (1 lb) chicken mince
1 red onion, finely chopped
3 cloves garlic, crushed
2 tablespoons chopped fresh mint
2 tablespoons chopped fresh
    parsley
2 tablespoons fresh lime juice
2 eggs, lightly beaten
2 cups (160 g/5¼ oz) fresh
    white breadcrumbs
2 teaspoons chicken stock powder
1½ cups (150 g/4¾ oz) dried
    breadcrumbs
oil, for shallow frying
4 large flour tortillas
lettuce leaves, for serving
1 large ripe avocado, sliced

Lime Hummus
300 g (9⅔ oz) can chickpeas,
    drained
2–3 tablespoons tahini
2 teaspoons sesame oil
2 cloves garlic, crushed
3 tablespoons fresh lime juice
1 tablespoon finely chopped
    fresh mint
½ teaspoon sweet paprika

1 In a bowl, combine the chicken mince, onion, garlic, herbs, lime juice, 1 egg, fresh breadcrumbs, stock powder and some freshly ground black pepper. Use your hands to mix thoroughly. Shape 2 tablespoons of the mixture at a time into round patties, dip in the remaining beaten egg and then toss in the dried breadcrumbs, pressing them on firmly.

2 Arrange the patties on a tray, cover and refrigerate for 30 minutes. Just before serving, shallow-fry the patties in moderately hot oil for 2–3 minutes each side, or until golden and cooked through. Drain on paper towels.

3 To make Lime Hummus: Process the chickpeas, tahini, sesame oil, garlic, lime juice and a little salt and pepper in a food processor until the mixture is smooth and has a thick paste consistency. Transfer to a bowl and stir in the mint and paprika.

4 To serve, toast the tortillas under a preheated grill or place in a dry pan until heated and lightly browned on both sides. Arrange lettuce leaves, a few chicken patties and some sliced avocado on each tortilla and then top with Lime Hummus.

Dip the patties in beaten egg and then coat with dried breadcrumbs.

Shallow-fry the patties for 2–3 minutes, or until golden brown.

Process chickpeas, tahini, oil, garlic, lime juice and salt and pepper until smooth.

LAMB, FIG AND BLUE CHEESE PIZZA

Preparation time: 30 minutes
Total cooking time: 45 minutes
Serves 4

1 tablespoon oil
2 leeks, thinly sliced
200 g (6½ oz) lamb mince
1 teaspoon ground cumin
2 tablespoons tomato paste

1 ready-made 30 cm (12 inch) pizza base
1 tablespoon fresh coriander leaves
3 fresh figs, sliced into wedges
200 g (6½ oz) blue cheese

1 Preheat the oven to hot 220°C (425° F/Gas 7). Heat the oil in a frying pan, add the leek and cook over medium heat for 10 minutes, or until the leek has begun to caramelize. Remove from the pan, drain on paper towels and allow to cool slightly.

2 In a frying pan, cook the lamb mince with the ground cumin over high heat for 5 minutes, or until brown, breaking up any lumps with the back of a fork or wooden spoon.

3 Spread the tomato paste over the pizza base, leaving a small border. Sprinkle over the leek, lamb and coriander. Then arrange the fig slices on top and cover with crumbled blue cheese. Bake the pizza for 20 minutes, or until the base is golden.

Cook the sliced leek until it has browned and begun to caramelize.

Cook the lamb with the cumin and break up any lumps with a wooden spoon.

Sprinkle the leek, lamb mince and coriander leaves over the pizza base.

CHICKEN AND PUMPKIN CANNELLONI

Preparation time: 1 hour
Total cooking time: 2 hours
Serves 6

Chicken and Pumpkin Filling
500 g (1 lb) butternut pumpkin, with skin and seeds
30 g (1 oz) butter
100 g (3¹/3 oz) pancetta, roughly chopped
2 teaspoons olive oil
2 garlic cloves, crushed
500 g (1 lb) chicken thigh fillets, minced
¹/2 teaspoon garam masala
2 tablespoons fresh flat-leaf parsley, chopped
150 g (4³/4 oz) goat's cheese
50 g (1²/3 oz) ricotta cheese

Tomato Sauce
30 g (1 oz) butter
1 garlic clove, crushed
2 x 425 g (13¹/2 oz) cans chopped tomatoes
¹/4 cup (7 g/¹/4 oz) fresh flat-leaf parsley, chopped
¹/4 cup (60 ml/2 fl oz) white wine

375 g (12 oz) fresh lasagne sheets
1 cup (100 g/3¹/3 oz) grated Parmesan

1 Preheat the oven to hot 220°C (425°F/Gas 7). Brush the pumpkin with 10 g (¹/3 oz) of the butter and bake on an oven tray for 1 hour, or until tender. When the pumpkin has cooked and while it is still hot, remove the seeds. Scrape out the flesh and mash it with a fork. Set aside to cool.

2 Add another 10 g (¹/3 oz) of the butter to a heavy-based frying pan and cook the pancetta over medium heat for 2–3 minutes. Remove from the pan and drain on paper towels.

3 In the same pan, heat the remaining butter and olive oil. Add the garlic and stir for 30 seconds. Add the chicken in small batches and brown, making sure the chicken is cooked through. Remove from the pan and set aside to cool on paper towels. Reduce the oven temperature to moderately hot 200°C (400°F/Gas 6).

4 Combine the pumpkin with the pancetta and chicken in a bowl. Mix in the garam marsala, parsley, goat's cheese, ricotta and some salt and black pepper. Cut the lasagne sheets into rough 15 cm (6 inch) squares. Place 3 tablespoons of the filling at one end of each square and roll up. Repeat with the rest of the lasagne sheets and filling.

5 To make Tomato Sauce: Melt the butter in a heavy-based pan and add the garlic. Cook for 1 minute, add the tomatoes and simmer over medium heat for 1 minute. Add the parsley and white wine and simmer gently for another 5 minutes. Season with salt and pepper, to taste.

6 Spread a little of the Tomato Sauce over the bottom of a large 12-cup capacity ovenproof dish and arrange the cannelloni on top in a single layer. Spoon the remaining Tomato Sauce over the cannelloni and sprinkle with Parmesan. Bake for 20–25 minutes, or until the cheese is golden.

COOK'S FILE

Note: You can use instant cannelloni tubes instead of the lasagne sheets. Stand the tubes on end on a chopping board and spoon in the filling.

Roughly chop the pancetta with a large cook's knife.

Finely mince the chicken thigh fillets in a food processor.

Scrape out the flesh of the cooked pumpkin and mash with a fork.

Combine the pumpkin, pancetta, chicken and other filling ingredients in a bowl.

Place 3 tablespoons of the filling onto the end of each lasagne sheet and roll up.

Arrange the cannelloni tubes over a little of the Tomato Sauce in the dish.

LAMB KOFTA IN RED YOGHURT SAUCE

Preparation time: 40 minutes
  + 30 minutes chilling
Total cooking time: 25–30 minutes
Serves 4–6

1 kg (2 lb) lean lamb mince
1 teaspoon ground coriander
1 teaspoon ground cumin
1/2 teaspoon garam masala
1 stem lemon grass, white part
  only, finely sliced
2 tablespoons chopped fresh
  coriander
1 egg
2 tablespoons cornflour
3 tablespoons plain flour
oil, for shallow frying

Red Yoghurt Sauce
2 red capsicums
425 g (13 1/2 oz) can crushed
  tomatoes
1/2 cup (125 g/4 oz) plain
  yoghurt
1 tablespoon sugar
2 teaspoons chopped fresh mint

1 Process the lamb mince, coriander, cumin, garam masala, lemon grass and fresh coriander in a food processor or blender. Add the egg, cornflour and some salt and pepper and process until blended.
2 Roll heaped tablespoons of the mixture into oval shapes and toss in the flour. Place on a tray, cover and refrigerate for 30 minutes. Lightly dust again with flour and shallow-fry in moderately hot oil for 2–3 minutes, or until just brown. Remove with tongs or a slotted spoon and drain on paper towels.
3 **To make Red Yoghurt Sauce:** Cut the capsicums into quarters, remove the seeds and membrane and brush the skin with oil. Grill, skin-side-up, until the skin blisters and blackens. Seal in a plastic bag or cover with a tea towel until cool. Peel away the skin and blend or process the flesh with the tomatoes, yoghurt and sugar until smooth. Transfer to a pan.
4 Heat the sauce gently, then add the koftas and simmer for 6–8 minutes, or until heated through. Stir through the mint just before serving.

In a food processor or blender, mix the lamb with the herbs and spices.

Shape the mixture into oval portions and roll lightly in flour.

Shallow-fry the koftas until just brown and remove from the oil with tongs.

When the capsicum has cooled, the blackened skin should peel away easily.

COUSCOUS WITH MOROCCAN LAMB

Preparation time: 30 minutes
Total cooking time: 50 minutes
Serves 4

2 tablespoons olive oil
1 large onion, finely chopped
2 cloves garlic, finely chopped
1/2 teaspoon cumin seeds
1 teaspoon ground coriander
1/2 teaspoon ground cinnamon
1/4 teaspoon ground nutmeg
500 g (1 lb) lamb mince
1 tablespoon chopped dried
    apricots

1 tablespoon raisins
2 tablespoons whole blanched
    almonds
1/2 cup (125 ml/4 fl oz) lamb
    or chicken stock
1 tablespoon honey
1 tablespoon finely chopped
    fresh parsley
300 g (9²/3 oz) couscous
2¹/4 cups (560 ml/18 fl oz)
    boiling water
2–3 tablespoons finely chopped
    fresh coriander

1 Heat 1 tablespoon of the oil in a large frying pan, add the onion and cook until soft and golden. Add the garlic, cumin, coriander, cinnamon and nutmeg to the pan and cook for 1 minute. Transfer the onion mixture to a plate. Heat the other tablespoon of oil in the same pan, add the lamb mince and stir until brown.

2 Return the onion and spices to the pan and add the apricots, raisins, almonds and combined stock and honey. Simmer for 40 minutes, allowing the stock to reduce. Season with salt and pepper, to taste, and stir in the parsley.

3 Just before serving, prepare the couscous by soaking in the boiling water for 5 minutes, or until all the water is absorbed. Season with salt. Top with the Moroccan Lamb and sprinkle with the chopped coriander.

Add garlic, cumin, coriander, cinnamon and nutmeg to the browned onion.

Mix apricots, raisins, almonds and the combined stock and honey into the mince.

Pour boiling water onto the couscous and leave to soak.

LEMON GRASS PRAWN SATAYS

Preparation time: 20 minutes
+ 1 hour refrigeration
Total cooking time: 15 minutes
Serves 6

1 tablespoon oil
1 clove garlic, crushed
1 tablespoon grated fresh ginger
1 tablespoon finely chopped
    lemon grass, white part only
1 onion, finely chopped
1 tablespoon tandoori curry paste

4 kaffir lime leaves, finely
    shredded
1 tablespoon coconut cream
2 teaspoons grated lime rind
600 g (1¹/4 lb) medium raw
    prawns, peeled and deveined
3 stems lemon grass, cut into
    15 cm (6 inch) lengths

1 Heat the oil in a frying pan, add the garlic, ginger, lemon grass and onion and cook over medium heat for 3 minutes, or until golden.

2 Add the tandoori paste and kaffir lime leaves to the pan and cook for 5 minutes, or until the tandoori paste is fragrant. Allow to cool slightly. Transfer the mixture to a food processor, add the coconut cream, lime rind and prawns and process until finely minced. Divide the mixture into 6 portions and shape around the lemon grass stems with wet hands, leaving about 3 cm (1¹/4 inches) uncovered at each end of the stems. The mixture is quite soft, so take care when handling it. Using wet hands will make the mixture easier to manage. Refrigerate for 1 hour.

3 Cook the satays under a preheated medium grill for 5 minutes, or until cooked through.

Add the tandoori paste and kaffir lime leaves to the pan and cook until fragrant.

Transfer the mixture to a food processor; add coconut cream, lime zest and prawns.

Wet your hands to make handling easier and shape the mixture around the stems.

BURRITOS

Preparation time: 15 minutes
Total cooking time: 40 minutes
Serves 2–4

1–2 tablespoons olive oil
1 large onion, finely sliced
500 g (1 lb) lean beef mince
1 cinnamon stick
1 bay leaf
4 whole cloves
2 cups (500 ml/16 fl oz) beef
   stock
2 teaspoons soft brown sugar
tortillas, for serving

Tomato Salsa
1 tomato, finely chopped
1 red onion, finely sliced
2–3 tablespoons chopped
   fresh coriander
3 tablespoons lemon juice
2 teaspoons grated lemon rind

1 Heat the oil in a large heavy-based pan. Add the onion and cook over medium heat until golden. Add the beef mince, cinnamon stick, bay leaf, cloves, stock and sugar. Bring the mixture to the boil, reduce the heat and simmer for 30 minutes, or until the mince is soft and has absorbed almost all the liquid. Stir the mince

regularly and break up any lumps with a fork or wooden spoon.

2 To make Tomato Salsa: Thoroughly mix all the ingredients in a small bowl.

3 Remove the cinnamon stick, bay leaf and cloves from the mince mixture. Use 2 forks to break the mince up finely. Serve rolled up in a tortilla with the Tomato Salsa.

COOK'S FILE

Note: The mince mixture can be made up to 3 days in advance. Cover with plastic wrap and refrigerate. The salsa can be made several hours in advance. Use flour or corn tortillas.

Add the mince, cinnamon stick, bay leaf, cloves, stock and sugar to the onion.

Simmer until the mince is soft and has absorbed almost all the liquid.

Remove the cinnamon stick, bay leaf and cloves from the mince.

PROSCIUTTO, VEAL AND APRICOT PATE

Preparation time: 20 minutes
  + 3–4 hours refrigeration
Total cooking time: 45 minutes
Serves 4

8 slices prosciutto
150 g (4 3/4 oz) chicken livers
350 g (11 1/4 oz) pork and
    veal mince
1 small onion, chopped
100 g (3 1/3 oz) dried apricots,
    chopped
250 g (8 oz) baby English
    spinach leaves, washed and
    dried
1 tablespoon finely chopped
    fresh rosemary
1 egg, lightly beaten
1 teaspoon seeded mustard
1 tablespoon plain flour
60 g (2 oz) pistachio nuts,
    shelled and chopped

1 Grease four 1-cup (250 ml/8 fl oz) capacity ovenproof moulds and line each with 2 slices of prosciutto. Preheat the oven to moderate 180°C (350°F/Gas 4).

2 Process the chicken livers, pork and veal mince, onion, apricots and spinach in a food processor. Transfer to a bowl and stir in the rosemary, egg, mustard, flour, pistachio nuts and some black pepper.

3 Press the mixture into the moulds, fold the prosciutto over and cover with greased foil. Stand the moulds in a baking dish and pour in enough water to come halfway up their sides. Bake for 40–45 minutes. Remove from the oven and water bath and refrigerate for at least 3–4 hours.

Lightly grease each mould and line with 2 overlapping slices of prosciutto.

Spoon the mixture into the moulds and fold the prosciutto ends over the top.

Pour enough water into the dish to come halfway up the sides of the moulds.

SAVOURY FILLED MUSHROOMS

Preparation time: 20 minutes
Total cooking time: 20 minutes
Serves 4

2 tablespoons olive oil
4 thin slices double smoked
   bacon, finely chopped
1 onion, finely chopped
1/3 cup (50 g/1²/3 oz) pine nuts
500 g (1 lb) finely ground pork
   and veal mince (see Note)
6 Kalamata olives, pitted
   and chopped

2 tablespoons chopped fresh
   parsley
2 teaspoons chopped fresh
   oregano
8 large mushrooms, stalks
   removed
1 cup (150 g/4³/4 oz) finely
   grated mozzarella cheese

1 Preheat the oven to moderate 180°C (350°F/Gas 4). Lightly brush the base of an ovenproof dish with half the oil.
2 Heat the remaining oil in a frying pan, add the bacon, onion and pine nuts and stir for 3 minutes over low heat. Add the mince and olives and stir constantly until the mince is just browned, breaking up any large lumps of meat with a fork or wooden spoon. Do not overcook.
3 Stir the herbs through the meat mixture and season well with salt and pepper. Fill each mushroom cap with about 3 tablespoons of the filling and sprinkle with the cheese. Bake for 10 minutes.

COOK'S FILE

Note: To grind the mince more finely, use a food processor or chop with a large, sharp knife.
Hint: Delicious eaten hot or cold with a green salad and crusty bread.

The mince can be ground up more finely using a large cook's knife.

Add mince and olives to the mixture and stir constantly until the mince is browned.

Fill each mushroom cap with about 3 tablespoons of the filling.

SEAFOOD QUENELLES

Preparation time: 30 minutes
 + 3 hours 30 minutes refrigeration
Total cooking time: 40 minutes
Serves 4

Quenelles
200 g (6½ oz) firm white fish,
 skinned and boned
150 g (4¾ oz) scallops, cleaned
150 g (4¾ oz) raw prawn meat,
 deveined
1 egg white
1 teaspoon finely grated lemon
 rind
½ cup (125 ml/4 fl oz) cream
¼ cup (15 g/½ oz) finely
 chopped fresh chives
1 litre fish stock

Tomato Coulis
1 tablespoon olive oil
1 clove garlic, crushed
425 g (13½ oz) can crushed
 tomatoes
150 ml (4¾ fl oz) fish stock
 or water
2 tablespoons cream
2 tablespoons chopped fresh
 chives

1 To make Quenelles: Pat the fish and seafood dry with paper towels. Roughly mince the fish in a food processor for 30 seconds, then process the scallops and prawns. Return all the seafood to the processor, add the egg white and lemon rind. Process for 30 seconds, or until finely minced.

2 With the motor running slowly, pour in the cream until the mixture thickens. Toss in the chives and place on a non-metallic or lined tray. Cover and refrigerate for at least 3 hours.

3 Using wet hands, mould about 2 tablespoons of the mixture at a time into egg shapes. Cover and refrigerate for 30 minutes.

4 To make Tomato Coulis: Heat the oil in a pan, add the garlic and stir for 30 seconds. Add the tomatoes, stock or water and some salt and freshly ground black pepper. Cook for 30 minutes, stirring occasionally, until thickened and reduced.

5 Strain the tomato mixture, discard the pulp and return to a clean pan. Add the cream and chives and reheat gently, stirring occasionally.

6 In a large frying pan, heat the fish stock until simmering—do not allow to boil. Gently lower batches of Quenelles into the poaching liquid, cover the pan, lower the heat and poach for 5–6 minutes, or until cooked through. Remove with a slotted spoon and drain on paper towels. Serve immediately with the Tomato Coulis.

COOK'S FILE

Variations: Instead of Tomato Coulis, you can serve the Quenelles with a white wine sauce. In a pan, melt 30 g (1 oz) butter, add 2 tablespoons flour and cook for 1 minute. Pour in 1½ cups (375 ml/12 fl oz) fish stock, stirring constantly until smooth and thick. Turn heat to very low and cook the sauce for 10 minutes, stirring occasionally. Remove from the heat, sieve and cover. Meanwhile, heat ¼ cup (60 ml/2 fl oz) white wine with 2 finely chopped spring onions in a small pan. Reduce the liquid to 1 tablespoon. Then stir in the sauce, ½ teaspoon lemon juice, 1 egg yolk, ¼ cup (60 ml/2 fl oz) cream and 1 tablespoon each of finely chopped fresh dill and parsley. Cook over low heat until the sauce has thickened. Pour over the Quenelles to serve.

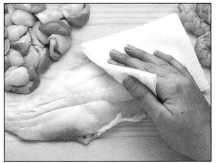

Use paper towels to pat the fish and seafood dry.

With the motor running slowly, pour the cream into the mixture.

Using wet hands, mould the mixture into egg shapes.

Cook the tomato mixture until it thickens and reduces, stirring occasionally.

Gently lower batches of the Quenelles into the simmering fish stock.

Remove the cooked Quenelles from the pan with a slotted spoon.

GOURMET VEAL SAUSAGE ROLL

Preparation time: 20 minutes
Total cooking time: 45 minutes
Serves 4

500 g (1 lb) veal mince
1 onion, finely chopped
2 tablespoons tomato paste
1/2 cup (40 g/1 1/3 oz) fresh
 breadcrumbs
200 g (6 1/2 oz) fresh ricotta
1/4 cup (45 g/1 1/2 oz) Kalamata
 olives, pitted and chopped

1/2 cup (75 g/2 1/2 oz) sun-dried
 tomatoes, chopped
1 tablespoon shredded fresh
 basil
1 sheet ready-rolled puff
 pastry
1 egg, lightly beaten

1 Preheat the oven to moderately hot 200°C (400°F/Gas 6). Mix together in a bowl the veal mince, onion, tomato paste and breadcrumbs.

2 Spread the mixture onto a large piece of foil to form a 25 cm (10 inch) square. Then spread the ricotta evenly over the mince square and top with

the Kalamata olives, sun-dried tomato and basil. Roll up the mince square like a Swiss roll, removing the foil as you go. Place the roll onto one end of the sheet of puff pastry and roll up the pastry to encase the mince roll, trimming any overhanging edges.

3 Place the pastry seam-side-down on a non-stick baking tray. Using a sharp knife, cut several steam holes in the top of the pastry. Brush lightly with the beaten egg and bake for 45 minutes, or until the pastry is golden and the sausage roll is cooked through. Pour off any juices before serving.

Scatter the olives, sun-dried tomato and basil over the ricotta.

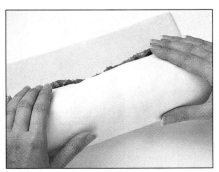

Roll up the puff pastry sheet to enclose the mince.

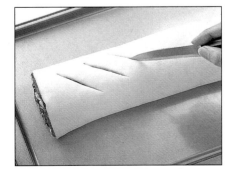

Score the top of the pastry several times with a sharp knife to make steam holes.

TURKEY BURGERS WITH CRANBERRY SAUCE

Preparation time: 30–40 minutes
Total cooking time: 20 minutes
Serves 4

Cranberry Sauce
30 g (1 oz) butter
1/2 small onion, finely chopped
2 teaspoons soft brown sugar
1/4 teaspoon mixed spice
1/2 teaspoon ground ginger
2 teaspoons grated lime rind
1 teaspoon balsamic vinegar

4 tablespoons cranberry sauce

500 g (1 lb) turkey breast fillets
2 tablespoons finely chopped
   fresh chives
1 egg, lightly beaten
2/3 cup (55 g/1 3/4 oz) fresh
   breadcrumbs
2 cloves garlic, crushed

1 To make Cranberry Sauce:
Heat the butter in a pan, add the onion and cook for 3–4 minutes, or until soft. Stir in the sugar, spice and ginger and cook for 1 minute. Add the lime rind, vinegar and cranberry sauce and simmer gently for 3 minutes. Remove from the heat and cool slightly.

2 Trim the turkey of excess fat and sinew, chop roughly and mince in a food processor for 20–30 seconds. Transfer to a large bowl and add the chives, egg, breadcrumbs, garlic and some salt and pepper. Mix with your hands until well combined. With wet hands, divide the mixture into patties.

3 Heat a little oil and butter in a large heavy-based frying pan. Cook the patties, in batches if necessary, for 3–4 minutes each side, or until golden. Drain on paper towels. Serve with the Cranberry Sauce.

Chop up the chives finely, using a very sharp knife.

Add the lime rind, vinegar and cranberry sauce to the mixture and simmer gently.

Cook the patties in butter and oil until golden on both sides and cooked through.

PRAWN-FILLED BABY EGGPLANTS

Preparation time: 15 minutes
Total cooking time: 35 minutes
Serves 4 as a first course

300 g (9²/₃ oz) raw prawns
50 g (1²/₃ oz) butter
8 slender eggplants
2 cloves garlic, crushed
1 onion, finely chopped
1 large tomato, chopped
1 tablespoon tomato paste
¹/₄ cup (60 ml/2 fl oz) white
   wine

1 Preheat the oven to moderate 180°C (350°F/Gas 4). Peel the prawns, and devein. Then chop the meat until it is finely minced.
2 Melt the butter in a frying pan, add the eggplants and cook in batches over medium heat for 5 minutes, or until soft. Remove and drain well on paper towels.
3 Add the garlic and onion to the pan and cook for 5 minutes, or until the onion is golden. Stir in the chopped tomato and prawn mince and cook for 3 minutes.
4 Cut the eggplants in half lengthways and place in a baking dish. Spoon the tomato and prawn mixture over the eggplants. In a small bowl, stir the tomato paste and white wine until combined and then pour it over the top. Bake for 20 minutes and serve immediately.

COOK'S FILE

Hint: Eggplants become fairly soft when cooked, so use a very sharp knife to cut them in half to prevent squashing them.

Chop the prawns with a sharp cook's knife until they are finely minced.

Melt the butter and cook the baby eggplants in batches until soft.

Place the eggplant halves in a baking dish and spoon the mixture on top.

CHICKEN TERIYAKI PACKAGES

Preparation time: 50 minutes + soaking
Total cooking time: 25 minutes
Makes 24

5 Chinese dried mushrooms
1 tablespoon vegetable oil
2 cloves garlic, crushed
1 teaspoon finely grated ginger
350 g (11¼ oz) chicken mince
1 small leek, finely sliced
1 tablespoon soy sauce
2 tablespoons dry sherry
1 tablespoon sake
1 tablespoon white sugar
1–2 teaspoons chilli sauce
100 g (3⅓ oz) fresh rice noodles, finely sliced
15 sheets filo pastry
90 g (3 oz) butter, melted
2 tablespoons sesame seeds

1 Place the mushrooms in a bowl, pour on boiling water and soak for 30 minutes. Drain and chop finely. Heat the oil in a large pan, add the garlic, ginger, chicken mince and leek and stir-fry for 4–5 minutes. Then mix in the soy sauce, sherry, sake, sugar and chilli sauce. Fold in the mushrooms and rice noodles and remove the mixture from the heat. Preheat the oven to moderate 180°C (350°F/Gas 4).

2 Unfold the filo, remove 1 sheet and cover the rest with a damp tea towel to prevent them from drying out. Brush the sheet of filo lightly with melted butter. Top with another 2 sheets, brushing each with butter. Cut crossways into 7 cm (2¾ inch) strips and spoon 1 tablespoon of the filling onto one end of each strip. Fold the ends over to form a triangle and continue folding to the end of each strip. Repeat with the remaining pastry and filling.

3 Place the triangles on a lightly oiled baking tray, brush with melted butter and sprinkle with sesame seeds. Bake for 12–15 minutes, or until a light golden brown.

Fold in the mushrooms and rice noodles and remove the mixture from the heat.

Place 3 lightly buttered filo sheets on top of each other and cut into strips.

Fold ends over filling to form a triangle and keep folding to the end of the strip.

107

MEATBALLS WITH FUSILLI

Preparation time: 25 minutes
Total cooking time: 35 minutes
Serves 6

3–4 slices white bread
750 g (1½ lb) pork and
    veal mince or lean
    beef mince
1 onion, finely chopped
2 tablespoons chopped
    fresh parsley
1 egg, beaten
rind and juice of half a lemon

¼ cup (25 g/¾ oz) freshly
    grated Parmesan
2 cloves garlic, crushed
¼ cup (30 g/1 oz) plain flour
2 tablespoons olive oil
425 g (13½ oz) can crushed
    tomatoes
½ cup (125 ml/4 fl oz) beef stock
½ cup (125 ml/4 fl oz) red wine
2 tablespoons chopped fresh
    basil
500 g (1 lb) fusilli

1 Process the bread in a food processor to form breadcrumbs. Using your hands, combine with the mince, onion, parsley, egg, lemon rind and juice, Parmesan, half the garlic and some salt and pepper in a bowl. Roll tablespoons of the mixture into balls and roll in the seasoned flour.

2 Heat the oil in a frying pan and cook the balls in batches until golden. Remove and drain on paper towels. Drain the excess fat from the pan.

3 Add the tomatoes, stock, wine, basil, the remaining garlic and salt and pepper to the frying pan and bring to the boil.

4 Reduce the heat, return the meatballs to the pan and simmer for 10–15 minutes. Cook the fusilli in boiling water until just tender and drain. Serve with the meatballs.

Combine the ingredients for meatballs in a bowl and use your hands to mix well.

When the meatballs are browned, remove from the pan and drain on paper towels.

Pour the fusilli into a large pan of rapidly boiling water.

SAVOURY BEEF GOUGERE

Preparation time: 1 hour
Total cooking time: 1 hour 20 minutes
Serves 4

1 tablespoon oil
1 onion, finely chopped
400 g (12²/₃ oz) beef mince
1 celery stick, finely sliced
1 small carrot, finely sliced
90 g (3 oz) mushrooms, sliced
2 tablespoons chopped fresh
    parsley
1 tablespoon plain flour
³/₄ cup (185 ml/6 fl oz) beef stock
2 tablespoons mango chutney
2 tablespoons fresh breadcrumbs

Cheese Choux Pastry
1 cup (250 ml/8 fl oz) water
100 g (3¹/₃ oz) butter
1 cup (125 g/4 oz) plain flour
4 eggs, beaten
1 cup (160 g/5¹/₄ oz) cubed
    Cheddar cheese

1 Heat the oil in a frying pan, add the onion and cook until soft. Add the mince and brown over high heat, breaking up any lumps with a fork. Mix in the celery, carrot, mushroom and parsley and cook for 1 minute. Stir in the flour and cook for another minute. Remove from the heat and stir in the stock and chutney. Return to the heat and simmer, covered, for about 30 minutes, stirring occasionally. Add a little water if it starts to stick to the bottom. Season, to taste.

2 To make Cheese Choux Pastry: Stir water and butter in a pan until the butter has melted; bring to the boil. As soon as the liquid begins to boil, add the sifted flour and beat well.

The mixture will become very smooth and leave the sides of the pan. Cool slightly. Transfer mixture to a food processor or small bowl and gradually add the egg, beating or processing well after each addition, until the mixture is stiff and glossy. Season with salt and stir in the cheese.

3 Preheat the oven to moderately hot 200°C (400°F/Gas 6). Lightly oil a large ovenproof dish, about 25 cm (10 inches) long, and spoon the pastry around the edge in a thick border. Spoon in the filling and sprinkle with breadcrumbs. Bake for 40 minutes, or until the pastry is puffed and golden.

Add the celery, carrot, mushroom and parsley to the mince.

For the Choux Pastry, beat the sifted flour into the boiling water and butter.

Transfer the mixture to a small bowl, add the egg gradually and beat it in well.

SPICY LAMB PIE

Preparation time: 40 minutes
Total cooking time: 1 hour 15 minutes
Serves 6

1 tablespoon oil
1 large onion, chopped
2 cloves garlic, crushed
500 g (1 lb) lamb mince
1 teaspoon ground cinnamon
2 teaspoons ground cumin
1 teaspoon curry powder
1/4 cup (60 ml/2 fl oz) red wine
1/4 cup (60 g/2 oz) tomato paste
1/3 cup (50 g/1²/3 oz) currants

500 g (1 lb) English spinach
    leaves, shredded
2 tablespoons marmalade
1/4 cup (60 ml/2 fl oz) beef stock
12 sheets filo pastry
80 g (2²/3 oz) butter, melted

1 Preheat the oven to moderate 180°C (350°F/Gas 4). Brush a 21 cm (8¹/2 inch) round pie dish with butter. Heat the oil in a pan, add the onion and garlic and stir for 2 minutes. Add the lamb mince and stir for 5 minutes, breaking up any lumps with a fork.
2 Add the spices, wine, tomato paste, currants, spinach, marmalade and stock. Simmer, uncovered, for

20 minutes, or until all the liquid has evaporated. Season with salt and pepper. Allow to cool.
3 Remove 1 sheet of pastry and cover the rest with a damp tea towel to prevent drying out. Brush the sheet of filo lightly with the butter and cover with another 2 sheets, brushing each with butter. Cut in half, crossways, and line the pie dish with the 2 halves of pastry, leaving any overhanging edges. Spoon the lamb mixture into the dish. Brush the remaining sheets of pastry with butter, scrunch each into a ball and place on top of the pie. Bake for 45 minutes, or until the pastry turns golden.

Add the spices, red wine, tomato paste, currants, spinach, marmalade and stock.

Cut the 3-layered sheet of filo pastry in half and line a pie dish with the 2 halves.

Scrunch the remaining 9 filo sheets into balls and place on top of the pie.

INDEX

A
Apple Yoghurt Sauce, 84
Apricot and Onion Sausages, 27
Apricot Pâté, Prosciutto, Veal and, 100

B
Barbecue Sauce, 56
Barbecued Sausages, 26–7
Barbecued Tuna Burger, 76
Basil and Coconut Chicken, 36
Béchamel Sauce, 52
beef
    Beef Pie, 7
    Beefy Potato Skins with Guacamole, 28
    Bruschetta and, 70
    Burritos, 82, 99
    Chilli con Carne, 39
    Cottage Pie, 34
    Crepes with Spicy Mince and Lentils, 32–3
    Eggplant with Filo Topping and, 31
    Goulash Soup, 14
    Hamburger with the Works, 9
    Herb and Onion Burger, 35
    Herbed en Croute, 79
    Indian Seekh Kebabs, 62
    Kebabs, 78
    Kidney Bean Burrito Bake and, 82
    Lasagne, 52–3
    Meatball Stroganoff, 30
    Meatballs, 56
    Meatballs Stifado, 71
    Meatballs with Fusilli, 108
    Meatballs with Tzatziki, 81
    Mexican Jalapeño Pizza, 49
    Middle-Eastern Chickpeas and Eggplant with, 64
    Mini Koftas, 78
    Moussaka, 44
    Nachos, 8
    Olive Balls and, 73
    Pizza, Red Capsicum and, 25
    Red Curry Beef Balls, 42
    Rissoles with Gravy, 17
    Sausage Rolls, 11
    Savoury Gougere, 109
    Savoury Mince, 23
    Spaghetti Bolognese, 10
    Spinach Curry and, 59
    Sweet Potato Turnovers and, 72
Bruschetta with Italian Beef, 70
burgers
    Barbecued Tuna, 76
    Chicken and Cheese, 24
    Cracked Wheat and Lamb, 76
    Hamburger with the Works, 9
    Herb and Onion, 35
    Turkey with Cranberry, 105
Burritos, 99

C
Cabbage Rolls, Stuffed, 43
Cannelloni, Chicken and Pumpkin, 94–5
Cannelloni Milanese, Baked, 54
chicken
    Basil and Coconut, 36
    Cheese Burgers and, 24

Dumplings in Green Curry, 74
Empanadas, 46–7
Lasagne, 52–3
Leek Pie and, 14
Lemon Meatballs and, 13
Lime Hummus Tortillas and, 92
Mushroom, Mince and Feta Strudel, 75
Orange Chilli, 86
Prosciutto, Veal and Apricot Pâté, 100
Pumpkin Cannelloni and, 94–5
Ravioli with Fresh Tomato Sauce, 90
Red Capsicum Terrine and, 87
Spicy Beans and, 36
Spring Rolls, 55
Tandoori Terrine, 29
Teriyaki Packages, 107
Middle-Eastern Chickpeas and Eggplant with, 64
Chilli con Carne, 39
Chipolatas and Spicy Sauce, 80
Choux Pastry, Cheese, 109
Cocktail Meatballs with Tzatziki, 81
Coconut Chicken, Basil and, 36
Coriander Sauce, 57
Coriander Sausages, Plum and, 27
Corn Husks, Fish Cakes in, 58
Cottage Pie, 34
Coulis, Tomato, 102
Couscous with Moroccan Lamb, 97
Cracked Wheat and Lamb Burger, 76
Cranberry Sauce, 105
Crepes with Spicy Mince and Lentils, 32–3
curry
    Beef and Spinach, 59
    Beef Balls, Red, 42
    Chicken Dumplings in, 74
    Spicy Lamb, 19

D
Dill Sauce, 56
Dim Sims, Combination, 63
Dipping Sauce, 50, 69, 73

E
Egg and Lemon Sauce, 88

F
Fennel and Chilli Sausages, Pork, 84
Feta Strudel, Mushroom, Mince and, 75
Fig and Blue Cheese Pizza, Lamb, 93
Fish Cakes, Thai, 51
Fish Cakes in Corn Husks, 58
Fusilli, Meatballs with, 108

G
Goulash Soup, 14
Guacamole, 8, 28

H
Hamburger with the Works, 9
Herb and Onion Burger, 35
Herb Sauce, 57
Herb Sausages, Fresh, 26
Herbed Beef en Croute, 79
Honey and Chilli Sausages, 27
Hummus, Lime, 92

K
kebabs, 62, 78
Kibbeh, Baked, 60–1
Kidney Bean Burrito Bake, Beef and, 82
Kofta in Red Yoghurt, Lamb, 96
Koftas, Mini, 78

L
lamb
    Baked Kibbeh, 60–1
    Couscous with Moroccan, 97
    Cracked Wheat and Lamb Burger, 76
    Fig, Blue Cheese Pizza and, 93
    Filo Pie and, 65
    Kofta in Red Yoghurt Sauce, 96
    Meatballs with Tzatziki, 81
    Mince and Polenta Pie, 91
    Mini Koftas, 78
    Pastry Fingers, 79
    Shepherd's Pie, 16
    Spicy Curry, 19
    Spicy Pie, 110
    Spicy Triangles, 45
    Stuffed Vine Leaves, 88–9
    Turkish Pide, 66–7
Larb, 40
Lasagne, 52–3
Leek Pie, Chicken and, 14
Lemon Grass Prawn Satays, 98
Lemon Grass Won Tons, Pork and, 69
Lemon Meatballs, Chicken 13
Lemon Sauce, Egg and, 88
Lentils, Crepes with Spicy Mince and, 32–3
Lime Hummus, 92
Lime Sauce, Chilli and, 57

M
Mayonnaise, Capsicum, 57
meatballs, 56–7
    Chicken and Lemon, 13
    Fusilli with, 108
    Stifado, 71
    Stroganoff, 30
    Tomato Garlic Sauce with, 22
    Tzatziki with Cocktail, 81
Meatloaf, Gourmet, 12
Mexican Beef and Jalapeño Pizza, 49
Moussaka, 44

Mushroom, Mince and Feta Strudel, 75
Mushrooms, Savoury Filled, 101

N
Nachos, 8

O
Olive Beef Balls, 73
Onion and Mint Relish, 62
Onion Burger, Herb and, 35
Onion Sausages, Apricot and, 27
Orange Chilli Chicken, 86

P
pancetta, 75, 94–5
Pastry Fingers, 79
Pâté, Prosciutto, Veal and Apricot, 100
Peanut Sauce, 57
Pide, Turkish, 66–7
pies
    Beef, 7
    Chicken and Leek, 14
    Cottage, 34
    Lamb and Filo, 65
    Mince and Polenta, 91
    Shepherd's, 16
    Spicy Lamb, 110
    Pistachio Stuffing, 20
pizza
    Lamb, Fig and Blue Cheese, 93
    Mexican Beef and Jalapeño, 49
    Red Capsicum and Beef, 25
Plum and Coriander Sausages, 27
Plum Relish, 18
Polenta Pie, Mince and, 91
pork
    Baked Cannelloni Milanese, 54
    Beef Kebabs, 78
    Combination Dim Sims, 63
    Empanadas, 46–7
    Fennel and Chilli Sausages, 84
    Gourmet Meatloaf, 12
    Herb and Onion Burger, 35
    Larb, 40
    Lemon Grass Won Tons, 69
    Meatballs with Fusilli, 108
    Prosciutto, Veal and Apricot Pâté, 100
    San Choy Bau, 48
    Savoury Mushrooms, 101
    Spicy Won Tons, 83
    Spring Rolls, 50, 55
    Stuffed Cabbage Rolls, 43
    Terrine, 18
    Turkey with Double Stuffing, 20–1
    Vietnamese Pork and Prawn Spring Rolls, 50
    Won Ton Crisps, 81
    Won Ton Soup, 41
Potato Skins with Guacamole, Beefy, 28
prawns
    Baby Eggplants with, 106
    Combination Dim Sims, 63
    Lemon Grass Satays, 98

Seafood Quenelles, 102–3
Spring Rolls, 55
Toasts, 80
Vietnamese Spring Rolls, 50
Won Ton Soup, 41
Pumpkin Cannelloni, Chicken and, 94–5

Q
Quenelles, Seafood 102–3

R
Ravioli, Chicken, 90
Red Capsicum and Chicken Terrine, 87
relishes, 18, 62
Rissoles with Gravy, 17

S
Salad, Spicy Pork, 40
Salmon Tartare, Fresh, 84
salsas, 58, 99
San Choy Bau, 48
Satays, Lemon Grass Prawn, 98
sauces
    Apple Yoghurt, 84
    Barbecue, 56
    Béchamel, 52
    Cheese, 44
    Chilli and Lime, 57
    Coriander, 57

Cranberry, 105
Dill, 56
Dipping, 50, 69, 73
Egg and Lemon, 88
Herb, 57
Peanut, 57
Red Yoghurt, 96
Tomato, 22, 43, 54, 90, 94
Yoghurt Mint, 13
Sausage Rolls, 11, 104
sausages
    Apricot and Onion, 27
    Chipolatas and Spicy Sauce, 80
    Fresh Herb, 26
    Gourmet Meatloaf, 12
    Honey and Chilli, 27
    Plum and Coriander, 27
    Pork, Fennel and Chilli, 84
    Pork Terrine, 18
    Spicy Tandoori, 27
Savoury Mince, 23
Shepherd's Pie, 16
soups, 14, 41
Spaghetti Bolognese, 10
Spinach Curry, Beef and, 59
Spring Rolls, 50, 55
Stifado, Meatballs, 71
Stroganoff, Meatball, 30
Strudel, Mushroom, Mince and Feta, 75

Stuffed Cabbage Rolls, 43
Stuffed Vine Leaves, 88–9
stuffing, 20
Sweet Potato and Beef Turnovers, 72

T
Tandoori Chicken Terrine, 29
Tandoori Sausages, Spicy, 27
Tartare, Fresh Salmon, 84
Teriyaki Packages, 107
terrines, 18, 29, 87
Thai Fish Cakes, 51
Tomato Coulis, 102
Tomato Garlic Sauce, 22
Tomato Salsa, 99
Tomato Sauce, 43, 54, 90, 94
Tortillas, Chicken and Lime Hummus, 92
Tuna Burger, Barbecued, 76
turkey
    Burgers with Cranberry, 105
    Pistachio and Pork Stuffed, 20–1
Tzatziki, Cocktail Meatballs with, 81

V
veal
    Baked Cannelloni Milanese, 54

Beef Kebabs, 78
Empanadas, 46–7
Gourmet Meatloaf, 12
Gourmet Sausage Roll, 104
Herb and Onion Burger, 35
Meatballs with Fusilli, 108
Meatballs with Tomato Garlic Sauce, 22
Prosciutto, Veal and Apricot Pâté, 100
Savoury Filled Mushrooms, 101
Stuffed Cabbage Rolls, 43
Won Ton Frills, 81
Vegetable-topped Mince and Polenta Pie, 91
Vietnamese Pork and Prawn Spring Rolls, 50
Vine Leaves, Stuffed, 88–9

W
Won Ton Crisps, 81
Won Ton Soup, 41
Won Tons, Pork and Lemon Grass, 69
Won Tons, Spicy Pork, 83

Y
Yoghurt Dressing, 64
Yoghurt Mint Sauce, 13
Yoghurt Sauce, 84, 96

INTERNATIONAL GLOSSARY OF INGREDIENTS

capsicum	red or green pepper	English spinach	spinach
eggplant	aubergine	coriander	cilantro
zucchini	courgette	thick cream	double cream
cornflour	cornstarch	cream	single cream
burghul	cracked wheat	sambal oelek	chilli paste
plain flour	all-purpose flour	silver beet	Swiss chard
prawns	shrimp	chickpeas	garbanzo beans
tomato paste (Aus.)	tomato purée, double concentrate (UK)	tomato purée (Aus.)	sieved crushed tomatoes/ passata (UK)

Published by Murdoch Books®, a division of Murdoch Magazines Pty Limited, 213 Miller Street, North Sydney NSW 2060.

Managing Editor: Jane Price **Designer:** Wing Ping Tong **Food Editor:** Kerrie Ray **Editors:** Kay Halsey, Wendy Stephen **Recipe Development:** Sally Parker, Kerrie Ray, Jo Richardson, Jody Vassallo **Home Economists:** Michelle Lawton, Kerrie Mullins **Photographers:** Chris Jones, Reg Morrison (steps) **Food Stylist:** Mary Harris **Food Preparation:** Christine Sheppard **CEO & Publisher:** Anne Wilson **International Sales Director:** Mark Newman

National Library of Australia Cataloguing-in-Publication Data. Fabulous Mince Recipes. Includes index. ISBN 0 86411 552 0. 1. Cookery (Ground Meat). (Series: Family Circle step-by-step). 641.66. First printed 1997. Printed by Prestige Litho, Queensland.